WILLIAM BLACKSTONE

Sage Of The Wilderness

Louise Lind

Published 1993 By

HERITAGE BOOKS, INC.

1540E Pointer Ridge Place
Bowie, Maryland 20716
(301) 390-7709

ISBN 1-55613-910-1

A Complete Catalog Listing Hundreds
of Titles on
History, Genealogy & Americana
Free on Request

TABLE OF CONTENTS

Introduction

At first, it seemed impossible. The Rev. William Blackstone seemed truly destined to remain a "footnote in history."

Then came a breakthrough. A one-paragraph entry in a biographical dictionary said Blackstone had one son who eventually settled "near New Haven." That meant descendants might still be living in the vicinity of New Haven. I wrote to a friend who also lives "near New Haven" and asked her to keep watch for the Blackstone name in the newspapers. I thought I might thus contact some one with useful information.

The day after my letter reached my friend, the *NEW HAVEN REGISTER* featured an article about the John Blackstone house in Branford, CT! I was able to reach the owner and, through him, Paul Blackstone, whose lifetime hobby has been collecting information about his pioneer ancestor.

Paul Blackstone, retired assistant postmaster of Branford made copies for me of numerous articles and pamphlets in his collection and graciously invited me to visit Branford. In that old seaport town on Long Island sound, I saw not only the John Blackstone house but the old cemetery where "John the Mariner" and his father, William Blackstone's son, are buried. He introduced me too, to Branford's beautiful public library, the James Blackstone Memorial Library.

Most valuable to me from Paul Blackstone's collection were the booklets written and privately printed in 1974 by the late Nathaniel Brewster Blackstone. A member of the New England Historical Genealogical Society of Boston, he seems to have done a thorough study of the Rev. Mr. Blackstone, subject of this book. Reading his works provided me with many leads for my own study.

Many aspects of William Blackstone's life remain in darkness. I am curious. Were his reasons for leaving England purely religious, or might they have been romantic? Did he come alone or with a retinue of servants? What were his themes when he preached to Roger Williams' followers in Providence, to the plantation owners at Cocumscussoc and to his eventual neighbors in Cumberland? Did he keep a journal? What did he and Roger Williams talk about? What were Blackstone's views about this struggling new colony? After all, he arrived here only three years after the Pilgrims landed in Plymouth and he participated in the first half century of New England's history.

I hope my little book will be of interest to visitors and residents of the Blackstone River Valley as well as to all who like to read about the very earliest days of American history. I hope too, that my work will promote scholarly interest in the Rev. William Blackstone. Perhaps there will be more breakthroughs, or maybe just a slow accumulation of small facts adding up to a more complete portrait of "The Sage of the Wilderness." I would like to see that.

Chapter One

BIRTH OF AN UNLIKELY PIONEER

By birth, William Blackstone was an English gentleman. By training, he was a clergyman and a scholar. By choice, he became an American pioneer.

Blackstone established plantations in what is now Boston and then, in what is now Cumberland, Rhode Island. He did so before any other Englishman appeared on either scene. He attained fame among later colonists as a grower of roses and apples. In fact, he developed the first North American cultivar of apples, the Yellow Sweeting.

"His taste in horticulture and woodcraft, and his skill therein and in all accomplishments of a similar nature, tend to confirm the conjecture that he was brought up on a large manorial estate," wrote a descendant, John Wilford Blackstone, in 1907.

The same writer points out:

> ... the chase and field sports which he, as the son of an English country gentleman, would have undoubtedly participated in, prepared his constitution to cope with the exposure and privation of a forest life, and gave him the knowledge and experience to obtain his food and take pleasure in its pursuit.[1]

The ancient Blackstone family, originally Norman French, possessed great wealth and honors. According to Robert Surtees, a 19th-century historian of Durham, England, the family reached the height of its prosperity under one John Blackstone during the reign of Elizabeth I.[2]

---

[1] John Wilford Blackstone, *Lineage And History Of William Blackstone*, Frederic, WI: published by John Wilford Blackstone Jr., 1907, 125 pp., pp. 79-80.

[2] R. Surtees, *The History And Antiquities of the Country Palatine Of Durham*, London: 1823.

This John had 15 children. The oldest, Sir William, (b. 1553) married Alice Claxton in 1581. It is to this couple that John Wilford Blackstone mistakenly ascribes the parenthood of the future New England settler.

Later and more thorough studies by Nathaniel Brewster Blackstone indicate that the future pioneer was a son of John Blackstone of Gibside and Agnes Hawley of Timberland.

In either case, he was a Blackstone, a member of that family of which Surtees wrote, "Few families of private gentry have spread more widely or flourished fairer..."

William Blackstone, the subject of this biography, was born March 5, 1595 in Gibside, the family manor at Whickham, Durham County, England. He was baptized in Horncastle Parish, Lincolnshire.

He had 10 brothers and sisters. One brother, Nathaniel (b. 1591), emigrated to America the same year William did. Another brother, John (b. 1594), was graduated from Emmanuel College and became a minister at Peterborough, England. Their oldest brother, Ralph (b. 1589), inherited the family estate. Siblings included also Frances (b. 1592), Ann (b. 1597), Muriel (b. 1599) and George (b. 1600). There seems to be no information about the three others.[3]

According to John Wilford Blackstone, Gibside was the most celebrated of the several beautiful estates in the Blackstone family. It remained in the family until the death of the last baron, Sir Francis Blackstone, in 1713. Gibside, he says:

> ... lies between New Castle on the Tyne, and Ravensworth Castle on Derwent water. Historians speak of "the beautiful and magnificent scenery which surrounds it." The park is four miles in circumference and the drive to the stately Banqueting House, seated on a noble elevation, is described as "through the bosom of a thick forest sometimes on the easy inclination of the hill, but still

---

[3] Nathaniel Brewster Blackstone, *The Biography Of The Rev. William Blackstone And His Ancestors And Decedents,* Homestead, FL: privately printed by Nathaniel Brewster Blackstone, 1974, 21 pp, p.1. Now on file at the New England Historic Genealogical Society, Boston.

embowered with venerable oaks." The gardens, the pasturage, the cultivated lands and the Mansion House itself were in keeping with the magnificence of the great park, and form together an estate and a home such as only a family of wealth, cultivation and distinction would possess and occupy... Such was the home and such the friends he (William Blackstone) left. [4]

Thomas Coffin Amory, in a paper he presented before The Boston Society on Nov. 9, 1880, says, "It seems reasonable to suppose that all of the name of Blackstone descend from the well-known stem in the Palatinate of Durham, the earliest of whom mentioned - Sir Hugh - was proprietor of Blackstone, about six miles from the Episcopal Cathedral City."

The way the manor named Blackstone... or Blakiston as it was usually spelled... was lost to the family throws light on how varied were the religious affiliations among the familial branches. John Wilford Blackstone goes on to say:

"The Blakistons were mainly Catholics even after the Reformation of the sixteenth century when Tudor governments diverted the nation away from obedience to Rome... The Rebellion of the Northern Earls was the first serious threat to the position of Elizabeth, and members of the Blakiston family joined it... It is also known that Marmaduke Blakiston, the brother of John, was involved in the Rebellion and actually composed some of the manifestoes... Unfortunately, his (John's) son, Sir William Blakiston - although knighted at Whitehall in 1603 - preferred to parade his Catholicism openly, and with disastrous consequences for the family... part of his estates were given to his brother Marmaduke by order of the Crown. It is known that he had to sell other lands in order to pay recusancy fines for non-attendance at (the Anglican) church... The dual process of land division and fines for recusancy... placed an intolerable strain on the Blakistons at Blakiston. It culminated in the decision of Sir Thomas Blakiston, first son of Sir William, to sell Blakiston Manor in 1615.

---

[4] Ibid. pp. 80 and 81

Meanwhile, on the other side of the political-religious fence, John Blakiston, son of Marmaduke, was a prominent Puritan and served as one of the trial judges of Charles I. This John Blakiston's name is on the king's death warrant.

Their future Non-Conformist cousin, William, studied at Emmanuel College, which was known at the time as "the Puritan college" because it was producing so many Puritan divines.

It may be well, at this point, to explain why there are so many ways to spell Blackstone.

In those days, spelling was not an absolute science. The same name might be spelled two ways in the same document. Also, names were often spelled according to the skill, the imagination or the "ear" of the scribe. Since the Blackstone family estates were in the north of England, near the Scottish border, and some members emigrated to Ireland, the spelling changed according to how "Blackstone" was pronounced by English, Scotch or Irish tongues.

Why, then, is "Blackstone" considered the correct spelling? John Wilford Blackstone gives the following explanation:

> There is on the border of England and Scotland, a range of hills called Blackstone hills. They are no doubt so named from the color of the rocks and cliffs which are found there... The family or clan owning or occupying the Blackstone hills would be known as John or Charles of Blackstone. In time, the preposition would be dropped and the family would take the surname Blackstone. We can thus determine among many forms, the true spelling of the name.[5]

Correctly or not, William Blackstone signed his name Blaxton at college and throughout his later life as well.

Today, the Blackstone family can trace its ancestry through more than 50 generations. The Sir William Blackstone (b. 1723, d. 1780) whose

---

[5] Ibid.

Commentaries On The Laws Of England so strongly affected the study of law in both Britain and the United States, is found among the branches of the family tree. He is not, however, a direct descendant of the Rev. Mr. Blackstone.

If one wants to find such descendants, one may find several living in Branford, CT. The Rev. William Blackstone's son, John, settled in that small port on Long Island Sound some time between 1692 and 1700. Twelve generations of Blackstones have lived there since. One of the Boston-Cumberland settler's two grandsons, William, settled in Maine. The other, called John the Mariner, made Branford his home port. Later generations spread to New York and across the entire United States. There are 1105 Blackstones listed in the 1989 edition of *The National Registry of Living Blackstones.*[6]

Burke's General Armory documents the Blackstone coat of arms. Significantly, both crest and shield feature cocks, implying that the family's vast estates produced fowl and the by-products thereof. The crest and shield would have served as the equivalent of a commercial trademark. [7]

This, then, was the noble family into which William, the future "Sage of the Wilderness," was born.

Blackstone family coat of arms

William's childhood, however, was not necessarily a happy one. He was only seven years old when his mother died, Dec. 8, 1602. His five-year-old sister, Muriel, died when he was 10. At age 14, he was sent off to Emmanuel College, Cambridge, to begin 12 years of study for the Anglican priesthood.

---

[6] Published by *The Blackstone Family News*, 930 S. Monaco, Box 11227, Denver, CO 80224.

[7] Nathaniel Brewster Blackstone, *Blackstone, Origin Of The Name, Coat Of Arms And Crest,* Homestead, FL, 1974. p. 7. "The Blackstone coat of arms is recorded in ancient heraldic archives, the documentation of which can be found in BURKE'S GENERAL ARMORY."

At the time of William's birth, Elizabeth I was in the process of completing the establishment of the Anglican Church.   While he was at Emmanuel, King James authorized the printing of the Bible in the vernacular. Blackstone was preparing to serve in a "new" Church.

In 1617, William Blackstone was granted a bachelor of arts degree. Four years later, he received his master's degree and in May 1621, in the diocese of Peterborough, along with his friend, William Morrell, he was ordained in the Church of England.

By virtue of this ordination, Blackstone became eligible for a benefice, an ecclesiastical office to which revenue from an endowment was attached. "Knights and beneficed clergymen abounded in the family," according to Amory (ibid.). His uncle, Marmaduke (b. 1555), was currently a deacon at the church of Durham and eventually was given the title of "dignitary."

Whether the newly ordained Blackstone was offered a benefice at this time or not, is not known. Perhaps even by then, he was known as an independent thinker. Or perhaps he was rejected because of his kinship with some of the participants in the political and religious battles then being waged in England. His brother, Nathaniel, for example, was said to be very close to the John Blackstone of the Long Parliament, the close friend of Cromwell and signer of King Charles' death warrant. For whatever eason, ejection at this time may have initiated William Blackstone's lifelong dislike for the "lord bishops."

Typical ship of the 17th century

Both William and Nathaniel Blackstone sailed for the New World the same year, 1623. [8] Nathaniel settled in Maryland on a large island in the Potomac River that became known as Blacki-stone's Island, then St. Clement's Island.

Did the two brothers leave their homeland for the same reason... because they radically disagreed with the religious and civic leaders of England? Possibly. Even probably.

"What was the real underlying cause of his self-imposed exile?" muses John Wilford Blackstone about William's decision to leave England. Certainly it was not because of any misunderstanding with his parents as some have suggested. His mother had been dead for 17 years by the time he finished his studies. His father died a few months after his graduation and ordination, three days before the new clergyman's 27th birthday.

"Powerful indeed must have been the influence, and urgent the conscientious necessity which compelled him to leave some of the fairest of earth's scenes and the intercourse of refined and cultured friends for the deep solitudes of the American wilderness," continues J. W. Blackstone. [9]

But leave, he did.

In midsummer of 1623, the Rev. William Blackstone and his friend and fellow Emmanuel alumnus, the Rev. William Morrell, were among the members of the Gorges Expedition aboard the good ship Katherine as she sailed out of Plymouth (England) harbor for the England that was "New."

As the Rev. Mr. Morrell later told Governor Bradford, Sir Ferdinando Gorges planned for him, Morrell, to establish Anglican "power and authority of superintending over other churches" in New England. The Rev. Mr. Blackstone was to be his assistant.

*****

---

[8] Nathaniel Brewster Blackstone was of the opinion that Nathaniel sailed on the same ship as his clergyman brother, the Katherine. The register of the Katherine, however, which lists William's name, does not list Nathaniel's.

[9] John Wilford Blackstone, *Lineage And History Of William Blackstone*, Minneapolis, MN: 1907. Published by John Wilford Blackstone Jr. p. 81.

Chapter Two

A WHOLE NEW WORLD

Sir Ferdinando Gorges was a courtier with grandiose ideas of carving a new England in the New World. His biggest obstacle was obtaining sufficient financial support. For this expedition, his second, Sir Ferdinando convinced King James to hold a drawing in Greenwich Palace to promote interest and investment on the part of other English noblemen. The nobles accepted the 20 fiefdoms into which New England was divided in the lottery, but kept their purses shut.

Nevertheless, Sir Fernando went ahead with his enterprise. He put his second son, Capt. Robert Gorges, in charge.

> ... When less than 30 years old, he (Blackstone) came to America with his friends Maverick and Walford, accompanying Robert Gorges in the expedition which left Plymouth, England, in the midsummer of 1623. This expedition represented the whole power and dignity of the council of New England.[1]

The following spring, Sir Ferdinando was obliged to send word to his son in Wessagusset, now called Weymouth, that funds at home were running dangerously low. Captain Robert Gorges and many of his fellow adventurers thereupon boarded the next ship back for England. Some of those who chose to remain, dispersed to better trading sites.

---

[1] Richard M. Bayles, editor, *History Of Providence County, Rhode Island,* New York: W. W. Preston & Co, 1891. Vol. II of 2 vols.

Before leaving, Captain Gorges put the Rev. Mr. Morrell in charge of what was left of the Wessagussset community.

The two clergymen, Morell and Blackstone, had little to do as far as superintending the New England churches was concerned. There was only one church. That was the Pilgrims' church in the four-year-old colony of New Plymouth, just a few miles south of Wessagusset. Since the Pilgrims had left England precisely to escape being "superintended", it is unlikely they welcomed any domination from Sir Fernando's two young emissaries.[2]

With time on his hands, William Morrell composed a long ode to New England, extolling her "fruitful and well-watered earth... and blessings rare." In the spring of 1625, however, he, too, chose to leave these blessings and return to England.

Blackstone, on the other hand, explored this "fruitful and well-watered earth" and, about 10 miles north of Wessagusset, found a peninsula that suited his fancy. One day, possibly right after saying farewell to the departing Morrell, Blackstone packed his belongings and headed for the harbor known today as Boston Harbor. If he went by boat - and that is likely - he would have rounded the peninsula the Indians called Shawmut, entered the Charles River, turned left into Back Bay and gone ashore on the western side of what is now known as Beacon Hill.

In 1625 Blackstone, "a bookish recluse," took up the lands on the Shawmut Peninsula, now Boston, and built the first house ever raised on that territory. It stood on the west slope of Beacon Hill, on land now bounded by Beacon street and Charles street, and faced the lands known as Boston Common. Here he lived alone,

---

[2] Bayles (ibid.) later in his book makes a statement about why Blackstone eventually left Boston which I have not seen substantiated elsewhere:

> ... He (William Blackstone) was hated because he was alleged to be trying to bring the established Church to the new country. He was charged with various crimes, his house was burned by order of the court, and he suffered numberless indignities.

trading with the Indians, cultivating his garden and watching the growth of his apple trees - the first orchard in the Bay Colony.[3]

The Rev. William Blackstone

Could Blackstone have been Boston's first Brahmin? He certainly fits Webster's definition: An intellectually and socially cultivated person regarded as aloof; esp: such a person from one of the older New England families.

He was intellectually and socially cultivated. He was one of the very first New Englanders. But was William Blackstone aloof? Was he, as so many early writers say, a recluse, a hermit?

---

[3]   Thomas W. Bicknell, *History Of The State Of Rhode Island And Providence Plantations*, Providence, 1920, Vol.I, p. 104-105.

Early records of the town of Charlestown state that when the Puritans arrived upon Blackstone's scene some eight years later, Blackstone was "the sole resident of Shawmut." That does not necessarily mean he was alone, however. Given his family background, it is likely that he had one or more English servants. He may have had Indian ones. Servants, whether of English or Indian nationality, simply did not count. His was the only household, that was all.

Too, there were English neighbors scattered around Massachusetts Bay..."stragglers" like himself, from Wessagusset.

Blackstone's neighbors were easily reached by boat. Thomas Walford, a blacksmith, lived near present Charlestown with his wife, Jane, and their two sons and several daughters. Samuel Maverick, who is described as "an educated, enterprising, hospitable man," lived in a fortified house near present Chelsea. David Thompson, an "agent of Sir Ferdinando and others," first settled in New Hampshire but then, four years before the Puritans' arrival, established himself on Thompson Island, near Dorchester.

The first American homes... like the first American colonists... were distinctly English in character. Taking advantage of materials on hand, Blackstone probably used rushes from Back Bay and The Fens (The former was a bay and the latter, swampland, in those days.) to make a typically English thatched roof for his cottage. Later, the snow of New England winters may have inspired him to build a sturdier wooden roof.

Blackstone had the largest private library in New England. He brought a number of books from England himself, and he may have acquired still more from his friend, Morrell, when the latter abandoned Wessagusset. Others of the Gorges Expedition who returned to England may also have left him some of their household furnishings, poultry, cattle, tools, seeds and cuttings from roses and fruit trees.

Blackstone's Beacon Hill home was no "Gibside" but it served him for a decade. Then he sold it and it lasted many years more. He may have built it alone, but it seems more likely he had help.

Besides qualifying for the title of Massachusetts' first orchardist, Blackstone early became known for his beautiful rose garden.

Andrew H. Baker, agricultural historian at Old Sturbridge Village, Sturbridge, MA, points out that this is not surprising:

> As a result of his education, he had access to the knowledge of horticulture and as a minister he probably considered it part of his duty to improve cultivation ... In the 18th century, many of the promoters of agricultural improvement in New England had clerical backgrounds.[4]

Old English rose such as Blackstone probably cultivated.

Blackstone's new home was on the sunny side of Beacon Hill. A spring of fresh water gurgled nearby. A meadow spread to the southeast for the cattle to graze on. In addition to his apples and roses, he no doubt planted a vegetable garden... a "kitchen garden," as it was called then. And no doubt he planted herbs for seasoning and for medicinal purposes.

His Indian friends must have introduced him to indigenous corn and

---

[4]   Letter from Andrew H. Baker, agricultural historian at Sturbridge Village,, Sturbridge, MA, to Louise Lind, author, dated Sept. 5, 1989.

pumpkins and the all-American bird, the wild turkey. The unpolluted bay and nearby streams were alive with fish.

Blackstone was probably leading a very pleasant life... quiet, but in tune with the seasons... a balance of physical labor and study, some traveling and no doubt some writing. Henry P. Dowst, in his *Random Notes Of Boston*, describes him as "a sort of Puritan Robinson Crusoe."

There are underlying indications that William Blackstone kept records of the Gorges Expedition of 1623 and the subsequent settlement effected by it. Nathaniel Brewster Blackstone says Winthrop alludes to this in his history and so do the *Proceedings Of The Massachusetts Historical Society*, 1878, p. 197.[5]

In 1628, Blackstone took part in the campaign to arrest the riotous Thomas Morton, a bon vivant who had divorced his wife in England and was making merry with Indian maids in the vicinity of Mount Wollaston. What really unsettled the other English settlers, however, was Morton's practice of bartering guns and ammunition with Indian warriors. Blackstone paid 12 shillings toward Morton's arrest.

There was other legal work to do, too. Alexander Young quotes Governor Matthew Craddock as writing in April 1629 that Blackstone, "a clerk," and William Jeffreyes, "a gentleman," were "authorized to put Mr. Oldham in possession" of land he had been granted by Gorges.[6]

I find Mr. Oldham's grant from Mr. Gorge (sic.) is to him and John Dorrell, for all the lands within Massachusetts Bay, between Charles river and Abousett river (Saugus River), containing in length, by a straight line, five miles up the said Charles river, into the main land northwest from the border of the said Bay, including

---

[5] Nathaniel Brewster Blackstone, *Biography Of The Rev. William Blackstone*, Homestead, FL, 1974, p.2.

[6] Alexander Young, *Chronicles Of The First Planters Of The Colony Of Massachusetts From 1622 To 1636*, Williamstown, MA: Corner House Publishers, 1978, p. 169.

all creeks and points by the way, and three miles in length from the mouth of the foresaid river of Abousett, up into the main land, upon a straight line southwest, including all creeks and points, and all the land in breadth and length between the foresaid rivers, with all prerogatives, royal mines excepted. The rent reserved is twelve pence on every hundred acres of land that shall be used; William Blaxton, clerk, and William Jeffrys, gentleman, authorized to put John Oldham in possession.

The sentence that immediately follows seems to suggest some high-handed legal practices on Craddock's part:

Having a sight of his grant, this I found. Though I hold it void in law, yet his claim being to this, you may, in your discretion, prevent him by causing some to take possession of the chief part thereof.

Blackstone was also said to have been empowered, in 1631, to put a certain Hilton in possession of land in Dover. Edward and William Hilton, sent out by Gorges and Mason, had established themselves with a group of merchants who styled themselves "The Company of Laconia" on the Piscataqua River at Dover, eight miles from the river's mouth where that other "Old Planter," David Thompson, had built his house.

The pageant of New England seasons may well have prompted Blackstone to write about nature. Henry David Thoreau a century later in nearby Concord had his Walden Pond, but Blackstone had the whole of Massachusetts Bay, Back Bay and the Charles River to inspire him!

In June of 1630, the solitude of the "Old Planters," was intruded upon. English ships began to enter Massachusetts Bay... By July 6, eleven of them were at anchor, some at what today is Salem and some at today's Charlestown.

The Lady Arbella, flagship of the Massachusetts Bay Company's expedition, was first to arrive. That was on June 12. Then, one by one over the next three weeks, other sails appeared on the horizon. From the top of

Beacon Hill, which was much higher in those days, Blackstone must have watched the ships maneuvering through the islands.

On July 8, the leader of these newcomers, Governor John Winthrop, called his one thousand fellow Puritans together for a solemn "Day of Thanksgiving" to God for their safe passage.

The neighborhood around Boston Harbor, Blackstone's neighborhood, was suddenly somewhat crowded!

*****

Chapter Three

𝕿𝕳𝕰 𝕳𝕺𝕾𝕻𝕴𝕿𝕬𝕭𝕷𝕰 𝕳𝕰𝕽𝕸𝕴𝕿

Blackstone lost no time in crossing the river to pay his respects to his fellow countrymen. Much to his delight, he found that his dear friend, Isaac Johnson, was among them. The two men had taken their college degrees together at Emmanuel and together, were ordained as deacons and then as clergymen of the Church of England.

A wealthy young man now, Isaac Johnson was married to Lady Arbella, sister of the Earl of Lincoln and the woman for whom the Puritan expedition's flagship was named. Johnson and Sir Richard Saltonstall, merchant and heir of the Lord Mayor of London, had been the most generous subscribers to the treasury of the Massachusetts Bay Company.

Most of the newcomers built their first crude lodgings at Charlestown. This is where Governor John Winthrop established his base of operations. This is where the first church was built. Since early in its history, the commercial company began to evolve into a theocratic commonwealth, the church became the seat of government.

It was soon apparent to Blackstone that the new colonists were not faring well at all. In addition to the expected vicissitudes of pioneer life, the settlers were plagued with persistent illness. Many placed the blame on the poor water supply. There was only one spring in the Charlestown area and its water was brackish. [1] People did not depend on wells for drinking water in those days. Their diet and discomfits on shipboard, followed by present deprivations of food and comfort may also have aggravated their problems.

Blackstone immediately invited the newcomers to cross the river and take advantage of the abundance of good spring water on Shawmut

---

[1]   The spring was near today's Bunker Hill Community College.

peninsula.

There is a tradition, related by Judge Samuel Sewall, a noted Bay magistrate who knew many of the early settlers personally, that Isaac Johnson was the first person Blackstone told about his "excellent spring" and that Johnson led the first Puritans over the river.

However, the Charlestown town records say that Blackstone "acquainted the governor of an excellent spring there; withal, inviting him and soliciting him thither." Governor Winthrop accepted and, the church records say its members "chiefly removed to Boston" early in August.

Anne Pollard, in her old age [2], recalled that she was the first Englishwoman to set foot in Boston. A child then, she had leaped out of the row boat that carried the first group over from Charlestown and waded ashore before the others. Was Blackstone standing there with a smile on his face and an apple in his hand to greet her? That is quite possible.

In later years, Anne Pollard and her husband, William, rented Blackstone's former property on Beacon Hill from one Richard Pepys.

What kind of people were these newcomers to Blackstone's neighborhood?

Historian John Harris, even while praising Governor Winthrop's dedication, calls his attitude toward democracy "shocking" to modern minds.

> The Bible convinced Winthrop there was "no such government in Israel" as a democracy. To Winthrop democracy was "amongst most civil nations, accounted the meanest and worst of all forms of government." Winthrop's view was precisely the widespread view of the (English) lords...: In any population "the best part is always the least and of the best part the wiser part is always the lesser."[3]

---

[2]   She lived to be 103.

[3]   John Harris, *Birth Of Boston*, Boston: 1980, The Boston Sunday Globe. p. 58, p. 63.

Harris points out that despite his conviction that "God had made some humans to be governors and most to be governed," Winthrop was consistently chosen as a magistrate in the Bay and was recurringly elected as governor all during the years when the Massachusetts Bay commercial company (which it was, at first) was being converted into a commonwealth." (Ibid. p. 58)

Eventually, the church of Charlestown - which means the seat of civil government as well - was transferred to Boston... but not immediately. The first court was held in the Charlestown meeting house on Aug. 23, 1630. A major piece of business was to put a ceiling on wages of "carpenters, joiners, bricklayers, sawers and thatchers." In spite of the fact that members of the building trades were much in demand, their wages were limited to two shillings a day!

Well-paid or not, the workers continued to add to the number of residences and shops on both sides of the Charles River. Isaac Johnson decided to build his Boston home on land adjoining that of his friend, Blackstone.

If Blackstone and Johnson had dreamed of neighborly relations between their two households, these were quickly and tragically dashed. At the end of August, Lady Arbella died. One month later, the 29-year-old Johnson, himself, died.

Lady Arbella was buried in Salem. Johnson, however, on his deathbed, asked that he be buried on his Boston land, close to his friend's property. He thus became the first man to be buried in what is now Boston's oldest cemetery, King's Chapel burying ground.

Blackstone's peninsula was quickly becoming a bustling little town. Although saddened by the death of his friend Johnson, Blackstone now had other Englishmen to chat with and shops to shop in. The Puritans, many of whom came from Boston, England, named the new community Boston.

At the General Court of Oct. 19, 1630, Blackstone and several of his fellow "Old Planters" applied for the right to vote. When they were admitted as freemen at the next General Court, May 18, 1631, the first to take the freeman's oath was William Blackstone.

Why did the new colony admit these "Old Planters"? For several possible reasons: to strengthen the colony's manpower, to recognize their long residence, or perhaps because some, including Blackstone, had obvious rights under the Robert Gorges patent claim.

The rules for citizenship in the Puritan community, however, became more stringent as time went on. Right after admitting the "Old Planters," the colony leaders voted that "no man shall be admitted to the freedom of this body politic but such as are members of some of the churches within the limit of the same." Three years later, the General Court of the Bay Colony of May 14, 1634 further stipulated that every person over 16 years of age, in addition to becoming a member of the church, must take an oath submitting "My selfe to the wholesome laws made and established by the same."

Blackstone was not ready for this. He continued to wear the canonical coat that symbolized his ordination as a clergyman of the Anglican church and pondered his dilemma for four years. Thomas Williams Bicknell, in 1920, described Blackstone's predicament thusly:

He is still an ordained minister of the Anglican church, in a measure a non-conformist, but not of the Puritan sort. To remain in the Bay Colony, he must subscribe to the freeman's oath, which demands full obedience to all laws ordained by a Puritan Church-State. He must also join the Puritan Church, thereby relinquishing his allegiance to the Church of England... Undoubtedly he made protests against what he called tyrannical laws, concerning which no record exists.[4]

Another problem surfaced. Some of his Puritan neighbors began to question Blackstone's right to his land. With their grant from King Charles in their hands, they felt they were entitled to the entire region. This, after he had invited them to share his peninsula!

---

[4]   Thomas Williams Bicknell, *History Of The State Of Rhode Island And Providence Plantations*: 1920, American Historical Society, Inc., NY, Vol. I, p. 106.

Blackstone declined to have his rights taken from him, saying in his independent and characteristic way:

> The King asserteth sovereignty over this new Virginia (New England) in respect that John Sebastian Cabot sailed along the coast without ever landing at any place, and if the quality of sovereignty can subsist upon the foundation of mere inspection, surely the quality of property can subsist upon the actual occupancy which is my claim.

Blackston's house at base of Beacon Hill

Quietly, he held his ground. He was willing to share freely the property he had purchased from the Indians, but he would not have it taken from him even by a sceptered hand!

It was becoming obvious, however, that he was no longer master of all he surveyed. All state and church affairs were dominated by the Massachusetts Bay Company and its governor, John Winthrop.

By 1634, Blackstone had had enough. He sold most of his land, reserving for himself his house north of Beacon Street and six acres around it. [5,6,7,8,9]

---

[5]   Before 1642, it is generally admitted that Blackstone sold his six acres to Richard Pepys. In Suffolk Deeds, 26,84, there is a deposition by "Anne Pollard, widow, aged about 89 years", that identifies the site of Blackstone's house as on present-day Beacon Street

(continued...)

Records show that each member of the Boston Colony paid Blackstone six shillings for his rights to the land. He bought some additional cattle and loaded their backs with his pots and pans, tools and clothing, seeds and cuttings, and his precious books. Alone, or with one or more servants, he

---

[5](...continued)

between Spruce and Charles Streets:

> This deponent testifieth and saith: that this deponent's husband, Mr. Wm. Pollard, occupied and improved a certain piece or parcel of land situated near the bottom of the Common at the westerly part thereof, in Boston aforesaid, and bounded on the sea south-west, for many years; and that her said husband had hired the same of Richard Pepys, late of Boston aforesaid, gentleman, deceased, who often told this deponent that he, the said Pepys, bought the said land of Mr. Blackstone, clerk, formerly of Boston aforesaid, and further that depondent saith that the said Pepys built a house thereon, wherein this deponent and her said husband dwelt for near 14 years, during which time the said Blackstone used frequently to resort thereto; and this deponent never heard any controversy between him and the said Pepys about the said land, but that it was always reputed to belong to him, as this deponent understood; and she further says that soon after the sale thereof, as she supposeth, the said Blackstone removed from this town of Boston; and further saith not.
>
> /s/ Anne Pollard
> Boston, Dec. 26th 1711

---

[6] John Wilford Blackstone, on p. 39 of his *Lineage And History Of Willian Blackstone*, 1907, says William Blackstone sold his six acres in Boston to Sir Henry Vane, who was governor in 1636. However, the Depositions, Suffolk Deeds 224.106 and 26.84 Gleaner Town Records 5.1-11 and 185 say he sold the six acres to Richard Pepys about 1635.

[7] In later years, these six acres were home to many distinguished Bostonians. Among them have been Copley, Channing, Harrison Gray Otis, Prescott, David Sears, Motley, Charles Francis Adams, Francis Parkman and others.

[8] Colony Records 1. 104 of April 1, 1633 state: "... to have 50 acres of land set out for him (Wm. Blackstone) near his house in Boston." The following year, we find in Town Records 1.2, "10(9)1634... The Town assesses 30 pounds to pay Wm. Blackstone for all his right except 6 acres."

[9] The broad meadow where Blackstone had pastured his cows, became by law in 1646, perpetually public property. This makes Boston Common, as it is called now, America's oldest public park.

set off again for a new wilderness, saying to his Boston neighbors as he departed:

> I left England to get from under the power of the lord bishops, but in America I am fallen under the lord brethren. I looked to have dwelt with my orchards and my books, and my young fawn and bull, in undisturbed solitude. Was there not room enough for all of ye? Could ye not leave the hermit in his corner?"

There is something wistful about this farewell. So short a time before, he had welcomed his fellow countrymen! So short a time ago, he had even offered to share his spring and his land with them!

It must have been with a heavy heart that he mounted his bull and took his place at the head of his domestic cavalcade. Indians meeting the procession on their forest trail, must have gazed in awe at the dignified clergyman astride his white bull, at his servant or servants, at the laden, lumbering herd of cattle... and at the pet fawn gamboling beside the solemn column.

The *Records Of The Colony Of Rhode Island And Providence Plantations*, p. 412, quote *Hist. Massachusetts Bay*, vol. i., p. 22, as summing up Blackstone's stay in Boston this way:

> At a point upon Shawmut, or Trimontaine, since Boston, lived Mr. Blaxton, who had left England, being dissatisfied there and not a thorough conformist; but he was more dissatisfied with the non-conformity of the new comers. He told them he came from England because he did not like the Lords Bishops but he could not join with them because he did not like the Lords Brethren. He claimed the whole peninsula upon which Boston is built, because he was the first that slept upon it. He had the grant of a very handsome lot there at the west part of the town, but he chose to quit all and removed to the southward, at or near what is since called Providence, where he lived to an old age.

******

Chapter Four

ANOTHER HOUSE ON A HILL

About 35 miles southwest of Massachusetts Bay, Blackstone came to the river the Indians called the Patucket. He paused where the Pequot trail crossed the sparkling, stream. He gazed at the salmon-filled waters and then to his left, where a hill overlooked the wide bend in the waterway. The site was both practical and beautiful. He would build his second American home here.

Blackstone called the hill Study Hill and named his home Study Hall. Here he lived until his death 40 years later.

Although he never moved from Study Hill, the site Blackstone chose was successively considered to be in five communities and in two states, eventually in what is now known as the Lonsdale section of Cumberland, Rhode Island.

When he first settled there, the Patucket River was the western boundary of Plymouth Colony. This area became part of the new town of Rehoboth. [1] Later, Study Hill was considered part of the so-called North Purchase, subsequently part of Attleborough.[2] Study Hill was within that part of Attleborough called The Gore, so named because its long triangular shape resembled the gore of a skirt. In 1746-47, Massachusetts ceded Attleborough Gore to Rhode Island and it became the town of Cumberland.

---

[1]   Rehoboth is where John Blackstone's birth is recorded. John was the only child of William and Sarah Blackstone.

[2]   The present city of Attleboro honors Blackstone as its first settler. A bronze plaque, designed by sculptor Norman Hines, hangs in its Museum of Industry.

It was spring planting time when Blackstone first arrived at Study Hill. Quickly he planted fresh shoots or cuttings from his Boston apple trees and from his imported English rose bushes. Quickly, he started another vegetable and herb garden. These were necessary if he and his household were to survive.

Sculpter Norman Hines chose William Blackstone as his first subject in a series of ten bronze plaques honering major figures in Attleboro's history.

Although he lived on the eastern side of the river, his plantation included land on both sides. The property on the western side was later within the jurisdiction of Providence Plantations.

> ... natural meadow was then considered the most valuable land... In the history of Blackstone much is said of his meadows on the river that bears his name, where he at once found an ample supply of grass for his stock of cows which he brought with him from Shawmut, now Boston. [3]

A couple of years went by. Blackstone was beginning to see the fruits of his agricultural labors. One can imagine him tending his farm animals, his orchard, his vegetables and herbs and beloved roses. Then one day, he

---

[3] John Daggett, *A Sketch Of The History Of Attleborough From Its Settlement To The Division*, edited and completed by daughter, Amelia Daggett Sheffield, Boston: Press of Samuel Usher, 1894.

received an invitation from the English colonists in Accomenticus, ME. They wanted him to serve as their spiritual pastor.

"This settlement (Accomenticus) had a definite connection with the Gorges group," Elfrieda Kraege wrote in a typewritten resource document on Blackstone in the Rhode Island Historical Library, Providence. "In declining this offer, he probably settled that he was never to become a full-time clergyman, probably feeling, as the letter indicates, that he had the 'expectation of farr greater profit by his husbandry' than he would gain by a clergyman's life."

... William Blackstone ranks with Roger Williams as a pioneer agriculturist, another preacher-farmer. At his 200-acres estate overlooking the river which bears his name, he is believed to have kept the first dairy cattle and to have planted the first apple orchard on land subsequently within the bounds of Rhode Island. [4]

Governer Stephen Hopkins

Eventually, Blackstone's work with his apple trees led him to develop America's first named cultivar, the Yellow Sweeting, an apple that in 1765, Governor Stephen Hopkins called "perhaps the richest and most delicious apple of the whole kind." Governor Hopkins went on to say, "Many of the trees, which he planted about one hundred and thirty years ago, are still pretty thrifty fruit bearing trees."

The Yellow Sweeting became popular as a rootstock and scions of it

[4] Carl R. Woodward, president emeritus of the University of Rhode Island, *Plantation In Yankeeland, The Story Of Cocumscussoc, Mirror Of Colonial Rhode Island*, a publication of the Cocumscussoc Association, Wickford, RI, published by The Pequot Press, Inc., Chester CT 1971; second printing 1985 by Narragansett Publishing, Inc., N. Kingstown, RI. p. 28

were distributed and grown throughout New England. It was still being grown commercially in Rhode Island in 1910. [5]

In choosing apples, Blackstone selected a crop that was much in demand. According to Goff (Ibid.) "Most apples grown in colonial Rhode Island and New England were used for cider, the universally popular beverage of that period. Vast quantities of it were consumed each year."

Woodward tells us that Blackstone "also raised hogs, and like other early settlers suffered from the depredations of the Indians, who found stray pigs easy game for pilfering. in 1635, the Indian Nahanton was ordered to give him two beaver skins 'for damage done him in his swine, by setting of traps.'" (ibid.)

The river, too, produced food for Blackstone's table. Bayles, in 1891, wrote, "Before the construct of dams upon this river, salmon were very plenty, so much so that they formed the chief article in the farmers' bill of fare." [6]

In Blackstone's day, the ford at the base of Study Hill was the principal entrance into the new Town of Providence from the north. 1 Bayles says (Ibid. p. 235):

> ... In earlier times this river had to be crossed by the first settlers of Providence emigrating from the Plymouth and Massachusetts colonies. Before the time of bridges, they had what were known as wading places. The first of these was at a place called "Ware," now Central Falls. The second was at Blackstone's "Wading Place," now Lonsdale; the third was at Pray's, now Ashton; the fourth was at Senetchonet island, now Manville, and the fifth was at Woonsocket.

---

[5]   Robert E. Goff, Department of Plant and Soil Science of the University of Rhode Island, College of Resource Development, *Apples From Rhode Island*, URI Cooperative Extension Service Bulletin 208, Kingston.

[6]   Bayles, Richard M., *History Of Providence County, Rhode Island*, New York. W. W. Preston & Co. 1891.

Bayles also reports, in the same book, that the river went by many names before it became the Blackstone.

> ... This stream... has been called the Seekonk, the Narragansett, the Patucket, the Neetmock, the Nipmuck, the Great, and, finally, the Blackstone. In ancient times it was called the Blackstone in honor of William Blackstone, but not until the beginning of the present century (19th century) did this name come into general use.

*****

Chapter Five

𝕿𝕳𝕰 𝕿𝖂𝕺 𝕿𝕺𝕷𝕰𝕽𝕬𝕿𝕴𝕺𝕹𝕴𝕾𝕿𝕾

Lechford hints at William Blackstone's habit of independent thinking in his *Plain Dealing*, [1] published in London only seven years after Blackstone left Boston. He mentions, too, another strong thinker who, although often of opposite opinion, became Blackston's close friend.

> One Master Blakeston went from Boston, having lived there nine or ten yeares, because he would not joyne with the church; he lives neere Master Williams, but is far from his opinions.

The "Master Williams" referred to, of course, is Roger Williams, the man on whom history heaps all the credit for founding the city of Providence and the state of Rhode Island.

Like Blackstone, Roger Williams had been ordained an Anglican clergyman, but at this time in his life, Williams' sympathies leaned toward Puritanism... his own version of Puritanism. While serving as minister to the Puritan church in Salem, he had gotten into trouble with the officials and was banished from that colony. This occurred about a year after Blackstone had his falling out with the town fathers of Boston.

In the dead of winter, 1636, Roger Williams left his wife and children in Salem, and fled into the wilderness to avoid deportation to England. He stayed first with Indian friends, then began a settlement in Seakonk with a few other Englishmen. [2] He received a warning, however, that this refuge was within the jurisdiction of Plymouth Colony and that he was still in

---

[1] Published in London in 1641 and quoted in *Records Of The Colony Of Rhode Island And Providence Plantations*, p. 412.

[2] This settlement was in what is now East Providence, Rhode Island.

danger of expulsion for his offenses. He promptly crossed Narragansett Bay and established himself at the head of the bay, the site today of the city of Providence. This was about five miles south of Blackstone's plantation.

John Wilford Blackstone, [3] poses this explanation of why Williams was expelled:

> ... Roger Williams was banished from Salem not because he was a tolerationist, but because he attacked the greedy land monopoly embraced in the charter of Winthrop and his followers. It was the same greed which made William Blackstone's holdings in Shawmut vanish away until with a faint show of justice, and after compulsion failed, they bought him out.

Upon reaching safety, Williams experienced such a sense of relief, he gave his new and permanent settlement the name "Providence." He said he felt there "a sense of God's merciful providence unto me in my distress."

Roger Williams statue in Prospect terrace,
over looking the city of providence.

Within the next 40 years, nearly 4,000 people established themselves in Rhode Island and Providence Plantations. These were English people of diverse religious persuasions, many of them Quakers, a sect persecuted by the Puritans with special wrath. Here, everyone was free to worship God in whatever manner his or her conscience directed.

John Wilford Blackstone (ibid. p. 57) was of the opinion that his ancestor, William Blackstone, deserves the credit for molding this motley group into a cohesive community:

---

[3]   John Wilford Blackstone, *Lineage And History Of William Blackstone*, Frederic, WI: published by John Wilford Blackstone, Jr. 1907, p. 57.

It was under the compelling will, the mental force and the tactful guidance of William Blackstone, who often addressed them, that these discordant elements were shaped and moulded until the whole colony stood squarely and firmly upon the platform of civil and religious liberty. It was Blackstone's thought, and Blackstone's words and Blackstone's example that were wrought into that charter that Roger Williams brought back from England with him.

The same writer continues:

Williams knew Blackstone well. He knew his mental training, his breadth of mind, his independent spirit, his dominant will, his piety and his humanity. When Roger Williams received his order of banishment, it was William Blackstone's voice he heard - the voice of one crying in the wilderness, and he went to him as to his leader... He settled... at Providence because Black-stone was there. Their relations were intimate, but they were the relations of the teacher and the pupil.

Unfortunately, we have nothing to document such a close teacher-pupil relationship and no testimony other than John Wilford Blackstone's that the Sage of the Wilderness had a hand in formulating Rhode Island's precedent-setting charter.

We do know, however, that Roger Williams often invited William Blackstone to preach to his own followers in Providence. On these preaching missions, Blackstone is said to have given Providence children "the first apples they ever saw."

Williams also introduced Blackstone to Richard Smith, proprietor of a plantation at Cocumscussoc popularly known as Smith's Castle. Williams maintained a trading post near Smith's Castle and often preached there to the Indians. For many years, the Williams family divided its time between this site on Wickford Harbor and its home in Providence. Roger Williams seems to have commuted to Cocumscussoc by water. He owned "a great Canow," a pinnace and several other small craft.

It is pleasant to imagine Blackstone and Williams cruising down Narragansett Bay in one of Williams' vessels en route to Wickford... perhaps munching some of Blackstone's apples as they pondered theological and political matters. History was being made in this new colony of England.

Sometimes, probably, Blackstone travelled the Pequot trail to Cocumscussoc on his bull. Overland, it was a distance of about 25 miles.

Richard Smith's Plantation house at Cocumscussoc. Known as Smith's Castle, It still stands near Wickford, RI.

Richard Smith's home was a gathering place for plantation owners of the Narragansett country. It was here they traded, conducted government matters and enjoyed social events. Although many were Quakers, there were also those who adhered to the Established Church and they asked William Blackstone to conduct religious services for them.

The religious importance of Smith's Castle and William Blackstone's role in it are documented in a plaque that hangs today in St. Paul's Episcopal Church, Wickford. The plaque is a memorial to Richard Smith, who died in 1666, and to his daughter, Katherine, who died "about 1664." It says in part:

> ... He (Smith) lived near Wickford at Cocumscussoc, commonly called Smith's Castle, and there Roger Williams often preached to the Indians and William Blackstone held the first regular services of the Church of England (of which there is record) in the Colony of Rhode Island.[4]

---

[4]   The farms in the southern part of the Colony of Rhode Island and Providence Plantations tended to be larger and more profitable than those in the northern part. Like some of his neighbors, Smith kept slaves.

Carl R. Woodward writes: [5]

> Cocumscussoc might... be called the springboard of the Episcopal denomination in Rhode Island. Tradition has it that the Reverend William Blackstone used to come riding his trained mouse-colored bull down the Pequot Path from "Study Hill," his country seat north of Providence, by invitation of the Smiths, to hold monthly services at their house. If, as is believed, the services were those of the English Book of Common Prayer, they constituted the first regular Church of England services, of which there is any account, in Rhode Island if not in all New England.

Like so many other individuals bonded by deep friendship, William Blackstone and his friend, Roger Williams were vastly different in character.

Williams was a fiery man, a leader of men, an organizer. Blackstone was introspective, a quiet man who, somewhere in his career, earned the title, "Sage of the Wilderness." There was something about Blackstone that made people think of him as "old" long before longevity earned him that title. Roger Williams, himself, described Blackstone as "the old man at Pawatuckquet" in an August 1638 letter to John Winthrop. Blackstone was only 43 at the time. Roger Williams was 36.

Both men began as Church of England clergymen. Roger Williams, however, soon became a Puritan, then a Separatist. In Providence, he established the first Baptist congregation in America. Only five months later, he resigned, saying he believed Christianity died when the emperors declared it the official church. He then became "a seeker," an unaffiliated person... a preacher to fellow seekers.

Blackstone, on the other hand, never lost his love for the rites of the Church of England. Symbolic of this is the fact that he was described as wearing his canonical coat even when he lived alone on Shawmut point.

Roger Williams was a family man. He had a wife, Mary Barnard Williams, and six children. Blackstone was a bachelor until he was 64 years old.

Although Williams loved apples, he never planted an orchard. He

---

[5]   On p. 28 of his *Plantation In Yankeeland.*

planted a city instead. [6] Blackstone was an orchardist and a botanist; a scholar and a contemplative.

Roger Williams was a political man and made several trips to England in behalf of the Providence colony. He finally succeeded in obtaining a charter assuring citizens that political affairs would be separate from state affairs and Rhode Islanders would be free to choose their own way of worshipping God. These were revolutionary ideas! Blackstone, on the other hand, does not seem to have had much interest in governmental affairs except to protect his property. He travelled regularly to Boston, Providence and Cocumscussoc but he never returned to England.

The two clergymen must have enjoyed many long and lively discussions about how things were developing in the New World. They agreed on that one principle that makes debate a joy: the right to disagree. Because they were true "tolerationists," they remained close friends.

We know William Blackstone preached in Providence and at Smith's Castle and Bertram Lippincott [7] says Blackstone preached in Boston in 1659 before Governor Endecott.   That was the same year as Blackstone's marriage.

On his own property in what is now the Lonsdale section of Cumberland, Blackstone had a tree to preach under, a tree that, in later years, was given the name of "Catholic Oak." By the time he was an old man, about 160 people had settled in the vicinity of Study Hill. It was to them, and to any Indians who chose to listen, that Blackstone preached under the oak tree's spreading branches.

---

[6] Professor Gough says Williams once made a peace offering of a bushel of apples and a glass of wine to a representative of King Philip. When Roger Williams died in 1683, Gough says, he was buried in a small cemetery just east of Providence's Benefit Street. "An apple tree grew near his grave. When his remains were disinterred in 1860, a root of the apple tree, in the shape of a human skeleton, was found in the grave. This great man... had been memorialized by the fruit he so admired." This apple tree root can be viewed, by appointment, at the John Brown House, Providence, headquarters of the Rhode Island Historical Society.

[7] Bertram Lippincott, *Indians, Privateers And High Society*, J. P. Lippincott, Philadelphia and New York, 1961, p. 29.

This tree seems to have been designated by God as a place for preaching. DeCosta (ibid.) wrote that the tree was still standing in 1880 and that it was dedicated to "universal toleration." He said a local clergyman several times held "divine service under its branches, employing the venerable forms loved by Blackstone so well." (pp. 23-24)

The Catholic Oak Tree. After the demise of this tree another oak was planted in its place.

The local clergyman was the Rev. James Cook Richmond, a "general missionary" for the Episcopal Church of Rhode Island. In 1843, on his way to a preaching engagement in Diamond Hill, the Rev. Mr. Richmond stopped under the tree and is said to have remarked, "What a beautiful tree this is. I think I will hold services here next Sunday." He thereupon entered the nearby home of Ezra Kent and wrote a notice to that effect, posting it on a board then located near the oak. The following description of the tree and its devotional use is contained in a typewritten paper dated Feb. 1932, stamped "Information Desk, Providence Public Library" and titled *The Catholic Oak, Singular Ministry Of The Rev. J. C. Richmond In Lonsdale:*

The oak is near the grave where the dust of the Rev. William Blackstone has lain for more than two centuries, and is only a short distance from the site of the new mill to be erected by the Lonsdale Company. Its base was encompassed over forty years ago by a sort of mound, and on one side were two large roots, which formed the sides of a hollow space. In this space, Mr. Richmond used to stand while delivering his discourse, and called it his pulpit... The first service was held on Whitsunday, June 4, 1843, and the service was styled by the reverend gentleman the "Dedication service of the Temple." He named the tree under which he delivered his discourse, the "Catholic Oak," which name it has retained to this day. This was the first open-air service ever held by the Episcopal Church in this country. Crowds of people attended, many coming from Providence, and it has been estimated that more than six hundred souls were in attendance...

... When he left Lonsdale (approx. 1847), he took with him an acorn which grew on the Catholic Oak, and carried it with him until he arrived in England, where it was planted. From it a fine oak tree sprang and is now flourishing.

In fact, the Lonsdale tree has a veritable clan-family in Europe, according to L. W. Russell, author of *The Native Trees Of Rhode Island*. He quotes the diary of the late Dr. C. W. Parsons, saying,

Through the agency of the Rev. J. C. Richmond, acorns from this tree have been distributed through many towns of Germany, and its offspring are thus propagated.

Russell goes on to say,

It has often been reported that the first Episcopal service held in this State was conducted under this tree. To get the historical truth concerning this, the author wrote to Bishop Thomas M. Clark, and received the following reply, which is certainly a valuable record:

Feb. 2d, 1900
Bishop's House,
Providence, RI

L. W. Russell, Esq.

DEAR SIR: - In reply to yours of the first instant, I would say, it has always been the tradition that the first Episcopal service held in Rhode Island was conducted under what is known as the Catholic Oak, at Lonsdale, under the Rev. Mr. Blackstone. The Rev. J. C. Richmond frequently held service and preached under this tree, and I have no doubt that he widely distributed the acorns from this tree, as is reported of him.

Faithfully yours,

Thomas M. Clark

There seems to be no record of exactly when Blackstone first preached under the "Catholic Oak," but his officiating at services in Smith's Castle are traditionally said to be the earliest in Rhode Island.

*****

Chapter Six

GOLDEN YEARS ON STUDY HILL

Some versions of the Blackstone family coat of arms display the motto, "Do well and doubt not." For the Rev. William Blackstone, a more apt one might have been, "Mind your own business." That, he did... to such an extent, some historians have labeled him a recluse.

That was not so. He did not exclude other people from his life. He cultivated friends; he traveled; he preached. It was he who invited the Puritans to settle in Boston and eventually he married. These are not the actions of a people-hater.

John Daggett said:

He was by no means a misanthrope, but a man of natural benevolence, who took this mode (departure from Boston) of indulging his love for solitude and securing the unrestrained enjoyment of his own sentiments and tastes. He did not shun man because he hated him, but because he loved solitude more than society. He was fond of study and contemplation, and here (on the banks of the Pawatuckqut River) he could enjoy both. His independent and original mind and character held nothing in common with the dogmatical and persecuting spirit of the age, and he determined to escape its presence and influence and avoid the theological controversaries of the day... He is said to have been devoted to his books, and though meditative in his habits, yet cheerful in his disposition. Though for so long a time a hermit, he was certainly not morose or disagreeable, and enjoyed intercourse with his kind if it could be peaceable. [1]

---

[1] John Daggett, *A Sketch Of The History Of Attleborough From Its Settlement To The Division*, Boston: Press of Samuel Usher, 1894, p.71.

Commenting on Blackstone's collection of books, Daggett wrote, (ibid.) "This library contained one hundred and eighty-four volumes, certainly a large library to be in the possession of a private gentleman of that day in the wilds of America." Alexander Young says that Blackstone had "186 volumes, among them three bibles and eleven Latin folios and quartos, which he probably brought with him from Emanuel College." [2]

Blackstone got along well with his neighbors, the residents of Providence, in spite of the fact that proper New Englanders of the time considered Rhode Islanders to be an unsavory crew. The Puritans of Massachusetts called Rhode Island "Rogue Island" because it was the haven of malcontents, outcasts and religious heretics. They looked upon Rhode Island and Providence Plantations as a sanctuary "for every false doctrine that stingeth like a viper." One reads that it was "the sewer of New England," "an asylum of evildoers," "a hive of hornets and the sink into which the rest of the colonies empty their heretics."

In 1643, when representatives from the three Puritan colonies, Massachusetts Bay, Plymouth and Connecticut, organized the New England Confederation, they excluded Rhode Island on grounds that it was unworthy.

In 1641, Lechford wrote, "At Providence... lives Master Williams and his company of divers opinions. Most are Anabaptists; they hold there is no true visible church in the Bay, nor in the world, nor any true ministerie." [3] Yet they listened to the Rev. Mr. Blackstone when he came to town to preach.

In spite of their reputations, Blackstone seems to have preferred to do business with his Providence neighbors rather than with the Rehoboth-Plymouth people. It was much easier to ride the five miles to Roger Williams' town than to journey through 40 miles of wilderness to Plymouth. Blackstone asked to have his land recorded in the Rhode Island colony.

---

[2]   Alexander Young, *Chronicles Of The First Planters Of The Colony Of Massachusetts Bay From 1623 To 1636*, Williamstown, MA: Corner House Publishers, 1978, p. 170.

[3]   *Plain Dealing* by Lechford was published in 1641 in London and quoted by Thomas Williams Bicknell in *History Of The State Of Rhode Island And Providence Plantations*, published in 1920 in Providence. Vol. I, pp. 105-106.

This may have been only the land he claimed on the southwest bank of the river, or it may have been all his land. In either case, we read in Records Of The Colony Of Rhode Island And Providence Plantations In New England, [4] "Ordered, that Mr. William Blaxton shall have libertie to record the right of his land in the records of oure Collony." This was in 1656.

Three years later, the following appeared in the same records:

By the Generall Assembly of the Collony of Providence Plantations, now mett at Providence. dated May 18th, 1659. To the much Honored, the Governor and Generall Court of Plymouth, in New England, These:

Whereas, Mr. Blaxton informeth that Mr. John Roome of Secuncke, hath an intent to possess a parcell of land neere unto the sayd Blaxton's, conceived to be within the bownds of our charter. The Court do order that Mr. Blaxton doe give notice to Mr. Browne to forbare takeing possession or makeing use of sayd land untill the lyyne and bownds betweene Plymouth and Providence collonys be agreed upon and sett; to which purpose the court have chosen Commissioners to treat thereof with Plymouth Commissioners. And further, the Court doe order, that the Clark of this Assembly doe give Mr. Blaxton a copie of this order to present to the aforesayd Mr. John Roome, of Secuncke, alias Rehoboth.

Thomas Bicknell (ibid.) adds that in 1666, Blackstone "petitioned the Rhode Island Assembly for relief from molestation as to lands by Mr. John Brown of Plymouth Colony and Mr. John Clarke was ordered to warnn that colony not to molest Mr. Blaxton in the quiet possession of his lands."

Occasionally, because of his better-than-average education, Blackstone was called upon to perform certain legal tasks in Providence. In 1655, for example, he signed the will of one Joshua Foote of Providence.

---

[4]   Printed by order of the Legislature; transcribed and edited by John Russell Bartlett, secretary of state, Vol. I, 1636 to 1663, Providence, RI; A. Crawford Greene & Brothers, State Printers, 1856, p. 341.

Apparently, though, Plymouth Colony continued to consider him one of its residents. Alexander Young writes [5] that the spot Blackstone selected "was then within the jurisdiction of New Plymouth, the government of which, in 1671, granted him the land on which he had settled, being about 200 acres." His place is mentioned in the 1661 records of that colony as that "where one Blackstone now sojourneth."

In 1667, a certain John Allen of Swansey laid claim to some part of the "West Plaine" which Blackstone claimed as his own. And a puzzling complaint appears in the Old Colony (Plymouth) Records: [6]

> John Allen Sen. of Swansey, complains vs. Mr. William Blackstone, in an action of the case, to the damage of L20, for molesting him in his just rights, by spoyling of his grass, pulling up of his fence, and destroying of his hay, upon his land which he had of the County, lying on the westerly side of the Western Plaine, from the said William Blackstone, which was done in the latter end of November, in the year 1667 - The Jury fined for the plf. six pounds damage, and the costs of the suite.
> Judgment was granted to the plf. according to the Verdict.

So contrary to character! William Blackstone does not seem to be the sort to go around spoiling grass, pulling up fences and destroying hay.

The matter was soon settled, says Daggett, the Attleborough historian. [7] "Allen did not appear, probably not recognizing the jurisdiction of the Court... We hear of no further complaint or interference." Would that we had more details about this!

It was officials from Plymouth Colony who, when Blackstone died, divided his 200 acres between his son and stepson. It was Plymouth Colony, too, that appointed guardians for his son, who was still a minor at that time.

---

[5]   Ibid. p. 170.

[6]   B. 7, p. 155.

[7]   Ibid.

DeCosta [8] was of the opinion that Blackstone did little in his lifetime to become wealthy. "It is... evident that he did not aim seriously at the accumulation of this world's good. Forty years of labor at Study Hill increased his personal estate only by that number (40) pounds."

There is no evidence that Blackstone was ever in want, either. He had

Blackstone the traveler

plenty to eat and plenty left to bring to Boston on Market Days, held every Thursday. He was held in high repute as an orchardist and cattle raiser. He must therefore have traded apples and dairy products for goods made in Boston or imported from his mother land. Too, there was game a-plenty in the forest surrounding Study Hill... wild turkey, quail, rabbit, pheasant, etc. There was an abundance of fish in the river that flowed through his farm. And Narragansett Bay, with its shellfish and other salt water bounty, was less than six miles away.

On one of Blackstone's regular trips to Boston... Was it the day he is reported to have preached before Governor Endecott?... he was approached by a young widow seeking his advice. Her name was Sarah Fisher Stevenson. [9] She had five children to support. Her late husband, John Stevenson, a shoemaker, had left her very little money. What was she to do?

---

8   Rev. B. F. DeCosta, *William Blackstone In His Relation To Massachusetts And Rhode Island*, reprinted from *The Churchman*, Sept. 25 and Oct. 2, 1880.

9   Sometimes spelled Stephenson.

Blackstone offered a very practical solution: Marriage. To him.

We have no record of whether the 64-year-old Sage of the Wilderness suggested this solution at their first meeting or whether it was an idea that, like one of his roses, had to bud before it blossomed.

There is no one to tell us if Blackstone had to woo the 34-year-old Sarah Stevenson on bended knee. We do know, however, that the Rev. William Blackstone took Sarah Stevenson as his wife in a civil ceremony conducted in Boston by his friend, Governor John Endecott, on July 4, 1659.

Who was Blackstone's bride?

According to Nathaniel Brewster Blackstone [10], Sarah was born in 1625, probably in England, and came to New England with her parents around 1630. She was 13 years old when her father died. At age 17, she married John Stevenson. By the time she was 30, she had given birth to six children. One died at about six months of age. After 16 years of marriage, John Stevenson died. At the time of his death, their youngest child, a girl named Sarah, was only three years old. The oldest boy was 15.

Bicknell [11] says Sarah Fisher Stevenson lived on Milk Street, Boston, on the site of a later building in which Benjamin Franklin was born.

A brief account of Mr. and Mrs. Fisher, Sarah Fisher Stevenson's parents, is found on page 167 of *Massachusetts Pioneers*: 1900, by Charles H. Pope:

> Thomas Fisher, carpenter, Cambridge, proprietor of house and land, 1634. Freeman 1634-5. Removed to Dedham. Administered property 18, May 1637. He died 10, June 1638. The town gave to his widow, 40 shillings, toward the bargain he had made in building the meeting house, 25, Jan. 1639. She paid

---

[10] Nathaniel Brewster Blackstone, *Biography Of The Rev. William Blackstone And His Ancestors And Descendents*, Homestead, FL, 1974, privately printed.

[11] Thomas W. Bicknell, *History Of The State Of Rhode Island And Providence Plantations*, Providence: 1920. Vol. I.

to the attorney, Elisha Bridge, 4, July 1639, a legacy left by her husband, for his daughter, Sarah, who married John Stephenson, about 5, December 1642 first then the Rev. William Blackstone 4, July 1659. Thomas' wife had leave from the General Court 13, May 1640, to administer her husbands estate, and to sell half of her lot for the bringing up of her children.

Why a civil ceremony? According to DeCosta, [12] the marriage of Sarah Fisher Stevenson to the Rev. William Blackstone

... took place five years before the time assigned by Drake as that when first "the Church service was performed in Boston without molestation," and seventeen years before the first Episcopal organization was attempted. Blackstone probably chose the services of the distinguished head of the Commonwealth in preference to those of "the Church" he would not "join."

We simply don't know whether the union between Blackstone and the Widow Stevenson was a romantic one or a strictly practical arrangement. It certainly provided benefits to both. Sarah had a place to live. And for Blackstone... well, a woman in Study Hall would certainly enhance the comforts of his home, something his age probably made him consider more than he did in the past. Too, with a comparatively young wife, Blackstone had a chance that he might, after all, have a son to carry on his name.

Here, we run into a mystery. The nuptial arrangements stipulated that Sarah's second son, 14-year-old John Stevenson, was to come to Study Hill to assist with the work on the farm. What happened to the other children? There is no record of their having come to live in the Blackstone household. Early records say nothing about anyone with the Stevenson name... other than John... having lived in the vicinity. Were they left with relatives or friends in Boston? This would not seem harmonious with Blackstone's reputation for loving children.

Nathaniel Brewster Blackstone, in his genealogical searching, came up with these meagre facts about the Stevenson children:

Onesimus, born Oct. 26, 1643, found work on a ship and was never heard from again.

John, born 1645, stayed with William and Sarah throughout their

---

[12]   Ibid. p. 17.

lifetimes and remained on the Blackstone property until his own death in 1695. He died a bachelor.

Paul was born Aug. 18, 1647. We know no more.

Joseph was born Jan. 23, 1651 but lived only about six months.

James was born Oct. 1, 1653 and turned up in Springfield, MA, at the time of his brother John's death.

Sarah was born Feb. 6, 1655 and thus was only four years old when her mother became William Blackstone's wife.

*****

CHAPTER SEVEN

FAMILY LIFE, TWO DEATHS

The Rev. and Mrs. Blackstone did have a child. In 1660, a year after they were married, Sarah Blackstone gave birth to a boy. In spite of already having a John in the family, 14-year-old John Stevenson, William and Sarah named this baby John, too.

With a wife and a new baby in the house and at least one stepson, William Blackstone's Study Hall was certainly no longer a hermitage! As his son grew from baby to boy, perhaps there were days when Blackstone wished it were. John Blackstone, it seems, was an unruly child.

Tradition runs that Blackstone early detected the fractious tendencies of his son, and observed that Solomon was mistaken when he said that a man could not know whether his inheritance would descend to a wise man or a fool. [1]

Perhaps realizing this son was never going to become a scholar like his father, Sarah Blackstone taught young John all she knew about her first husband's craft, "that of how to skin animals, the preparing of hides, and the making of all kinds of leather goods, as primarily footwear, but also saddles, harness, head gear, gloves, etc." [2]

---

[1] From the Rev. B. F. DeCosta's articles in the Sept. 25 and Oct. 2, 1880 issues of *The Churchman*, "William Blackstone In His Relation to Massachusetts and Rhode Island."

[2] Nathaniel Brewster Blackstone, *The Life Of John Blackstone, 1660-1743*, Homestead, FL, 1974.

There is a legend that William and Sarah Blackstone also had a daughter. John Daggett [3] tells the romantic story but, even while telling it, refutes it:

> It was long believed that Blackstone had an only daughter who was borne away from the abodes of society, - educated by her father alone, - who had grown up in communion with nature and was graced with the simplicity of nature's charms, a child of the forest and the field, a flower of the wilderness; and it was supposed she married John Stevenson. This statement is erroneously made in the Massachusetts Historical Collection. This was a too tempting subject for the novelist. In a fictitious work in two volumes published many years ago and called "Humors of Utopia," a daughter of Blackstone was one of the principal characters. It seems almost sacrilege to lay violent hands on such a picture. But in this matter-of-fact world "the gay frost-work of fancy" must often be dissolved by the light of truth. She had no existence except in imagination. In the old records, John Stevenson is called the son-in-law of Blackstone instead of stepson, and that is the only foundation for the supposition regarding his daughter."

There was a Sarah Stevenson, of course, but she was John Stevenson's little sister... not his wife.

One hopes that William Blackstone's household, when he brought his bride to it, still numbered some English or Indian servants. The lot of a pioneer housewife was not an easy one.

The ingredients for roast beef, turkey, goose, chicken or pork dinners were there for the taking, but one had to kill and dress the animal or bird before roasting its meat in the fire. The dairy herd provided milk for cheese and butter, but first one had to milk the cows and process the results. Port

---

[3]   John Daggett, *A Sketch Of The History Of Attleborough From Its Settlement To The Division,* Boston: Press of Samuel Usher, 1894.

wine and especially "hard" apple cider were common drinks, but one had to harvest the grapes and apples, press them and store their liquors until they were aged to an acceptable degree. There was beer to be brewed, too.

A typical kitchen fireplace in use at the time of Sarah Blackstone

"In early colonial days the custom of drinking liquor, a habit left over from the mother country, was common to all classes, and to all men, women and children. Beer was on the table as regularly as bread," says Edward Field. [4]

Susan Marie Boucher has this to say about the materials women of Sarah Blackstone's time worked with. [5]

Fish, a favorite food of the English, was always very plentiful. Lobsters, crabs, clams and oysters were also enjoyed in the colonial home. Following fish, Indian corn was in unending abundance and prepared in many ways, in breads, puddings, porridge and cakes. Because it was easily adaptable, it was frequently dried and brought along on long journeys as a major source of nourishment. Mixed with snow or water before cooking, it became a "journey cake" - now the famous Rhode Island Johnny Cake.

[4]   Edward Field, *The Colonial Tavern*, Providence: 1897, p. 10.

[5]   Susan Marie Boucher, *The History Of Pawtucket* 1635-1986, The Pawtucket Public Library and The Pawtucket Centennial Committee, 1986, printed by Arcata Graphics/Halliday Lithograph, West Hanover, MA. p. 19.

Oats were also raised, and a New England dish made of oatmeal, sugar and spice and a "pottle of milk" (two quarts), was popular. Pumpkin was another very bountiful crop, and it was used in as many ways as possible in breads, pies, sauces and stews.

Boucher also mentions that the passenger pigeons that migrated over New England every year were greatly relished. Over the years they were shot in such abundance, they became extinct.

Mrs. Blackstone, or the servants under her supervision, had other chores, too. They had to shear sheep, card and comb and spin the wool and weave it into cloth. Flax had to be harvested, pounded and spun into linen. Medicines had to be made from herbs. Soap had to be manufactured from meat grease and lye. And, of course, the supply of candles had to be kept up. These were made from beeswax or from the wax of bayberries that grew abundantly in this part of New England.

One wonders if Sarah Blackstone had time for social life. Did she sometimes accompany her husband on his trips to Mr. and Mrs. Richard Smith's "castle" in Cocumscussoc? Did they sail the Narragansett Bay in Roger Williams' pinnace? Was Mrs. Roger Williams as close a friend to Sarah as the Rev. Mr. Williams was to her husband? Mary Williams is said to have once visited the village of Limerock to see the quarry there. Did she ever visit Study Hill? Did she and Sarah Blackstone sip English tea together?

Fourteen years after marrying Blackstone, Sarah died. The records of Rehoboth state that "Mrs. Sarah Blackstone, the wife of Mr. William Blackstone, buried about the middle of June 1673." [6] She was 48 years old. She was said to have been buried not far from Study Hall.

The next two years must have been sad ones for the Rev. William Blackstone. He had lost his wife. He was nearing 80 years of age. He had a rambunctious, teenage son. And he was concerned about his friends, the

---

[6]   In colonial days, it was not unusual to record the date of burial rather than the date of death. Lorenzo Blackstone of Norwich states that her death is recorded in Hist. Coll. XX, 171.

Indians. Rumors of war were rampant. The Pequots of Connecticut and the Nipmucs of Massachusetts were causing him most concern, but even the Narragansetts, with whom he was most friendly, were beginning to finger their tomahawks, provoked by the cruelty of Blackstone's fellow Englishmen.

On May 26, 1675, just short of two years after Sarah's death, William Blackstone passed on to his reward.

Roger Williams wrote of the event in such detail, it suggests the possibility that he was present at the demise of his friend. In a letter to John Winthrop on June 13, Williams wrote:

> About a fortnight since, your old acquaintance, Mr. Blackstone departed this life in the four-score years of his age: four days before his death he had a great paine in his breast and back and bowels; afterwards he said he was well, had no paines, and should live; but he grew fainter and yealded up his spirit without a groane.

Sylvanus Chace Newman says "circumstantial evidence and expressions in records not easily accounted for in any other way" point to the presence at least, of both Roger Williams and Gregory Dexter, both clergymen and friends of Blackstone, at Blackstone's funeral rites. He feels they "no doubt manifested that respect which educated men like themselves would do at the decease of this learned and venerable patriarch."[7]

On the same day of Blackstone's burial, May 28, [8] "Mr. (Stephen) Nathaniel Paine and others of Rehoboth" took an inventory of his "lands, goods and chattels" and recorded the same in Plymouth Colony. "This was

---

[7]   S. C. Newman, A.M., member of the Rhode Island Historical Society, Honorary Member of the Dorchester Historical and Antiquarian Society, and Genealogical Secretary of the Blackstone Monument Association, *Dexter Genealogy: Being A Record Of The Families Descended From Rev. Gregory Dexter; With Notes And Biographical Sketches Of Each Parent*, Providence: Printed by A. Crawford Greene, 1859.

[8]   William Blackstone died Wednesday, May 21 and was buried Friday, May 28, 1675, Old Style. These dates correspond in New Style, to Sunday, June 6, and Tuesday, June 8.

taken but two days after his death, and was a common practice, owing to the condition of the times," says Bliss in his *History Of Rehoboth*.

Blackstone's real estate consisted of "Sixty acres of land, and two shares in meadows in Providence. The west plain, the south plain and land about the house and orchard, amounting to two hundred acres, and the meadow called Blackstone's Meadow."

His personal property, however, is what is most intriguing. This was his personal library:

3 Bibles, 10s; 6 English books in folios, £2	£2 10s
3 Latin books, in folio, 15s; 3 do., large quarto, £2	2 15s
15 small quarto, £1 17s. 6d; 14 small do., 14s	2 11s 6d
30 large octavo, £4; 25 small do., £1 5s	5 5s
22 duodecimo	1 13s
53 small do., of little value	13s
10 paper books	5s

£15 12s 6d

Remainder personal 40 11s

Total personal £56 3s 6d

The Rehoboth officials obviously did not place much worth on Blackstone's books. Today, however, they would be treasured by historians, especially if some of them were his journals!

*****

Chapter Eight

JOHN STEVENSON, STEPSON

With grim dispatch, William Blackstone's anxiety about a possible Indian war turned into flaming reality.

On June 2... Blackstone's body was hardly cold in the ground ... a band of King Philip's warriors invaded his plantation. They burned everything, including Study Hall and all its books. The earth itself was all that remained... the earth, a few smoldering ashes and two rough quartz grave markers.

Daggett [1] voices the difficulty this Indian raid creates for would-be biographers:

> The historian will always painfully regret the destruction of those "paper books," which were probably manuscripts, and must have contained the meditations of this solitary thinker, and might have revealed the mysteries of his strange residence in the New World. What a treasure was lost... We know his was a mind and spirit which could not brook the tyranny of men; but what other causes than those known, if any, contributed to his removal to this country will probably always be a profound secret.

Nathaniel Brewster Blackstone [2] wonders if things would have been different had the "lord of the manor" still been alive.

---

[1]   John Daggett, *A Sketch Of The History Of Attleborough From Its Settlement To The Division*, Boston: Press of Samuel Usher, 1894.

[2]   Page ii of the Epilogue of his *Biography Of The Reverend William Blackstone*, 1974, Homestead, FL.

It is... possible, though hardly probable, that had he not died when he did, he and his family might have escaped harm at the hands of King Philip's men...

William never seemed to have had trouble with the Indians. He had lived all his life among them and, speaking their language, he understood their character. Apparently, he possessed that faculty of morally impressing himself on primitive natures, which has been so highly developed in African explorers of the Livingston type.

One wonders how 30-year-old John Stevenson and his half brother, 15-year-old John Blackstone, survived so devastating a raid.

It is possible they were in Plymouth, settling William Blackstone's estate. On the day before the Indians demolished Study Hall, the following was entered in the records of Plymouth Colony:

June 1, 1675, Lieut. Hunt, Ensign Smith, and Daniel Smith are appointed and authorized by the Court to take some present care of the estate of William Blackstone, deceased, and of his son now left by him, and to see that, at the next Court, he do propose a man to the Court to be his guardian, which, in case he do neglect, the Court will then see cause to make choice of one for him.

A little over a month later, on July 10, 1675, the same Plymouth Court issued the following order in behalf of John Stevenson:

Whereas the Court is informed that one, whose name is John Stevenson, step-son to William Blackstone, late deceased, was very helpful to his step-father and mother, and in their lifetime without whom they could not have subsisted, as to a good help and instrument thereof, and he is now left in a low and mean condition, and never was in any manner recompensed for his good service aforesaid; and if (as it is said at least) his step-father engaged to his mother, at his marriage with her, that he should be considered with a competency of land out of the said Blackstone's land then lived on, which hath never yet been performed; and forasmuch as the personal estate of said William Blackstone is so small and inconsiderable, that he, the said Stevenson, cannot be relieved out of it; this Court therefore, in consideration of the premises, do order and dispose fifty acres of land unto the said John Stevenson out of the lands of the said William Blackstone and five acres of meadow, to be laid out unto him by Ensign Henry Smith, Mr. Daniel Smith and Mr. Nathaniel Paine, according as they shall think meet so as it may be most commodious to him, or as little prejudicial to the seat of Mr. William Blackstone as may be. By order of the Court for the jurisdiction of Plymouth.

It is interesting to note that, even though Blackstone had close ties to Providence, it was the Plymouth Colony that exerted jurisdiction over his property and his son even after his death. This record raises many questions, however.

Was Blackstone's land divided at John Stevenson's request? It is unlikely that the Plymouth Court, on its own, would initiate such a case. Some say Paine and the Smiths, both prominent men in the Rehoboth part of Plymouth Colony, were friends of Stevenson. Did they conspire to benefit Stevenson at the expense of John Blackstone? Or was it simply an effort on the parts of the Smiths and Paine to give John Stevenson his just reward?

What does the document mean when it describes William Blackstone's personal estate as "small and inconsiderable?"

Would the Rev. Mr. Blackstone have given John Stevenson a block of his land had he gotten around to it? Perhaps he had written this into a will and mentioned it to his stepson. Was the will overlooked among his books when the inventory was taken? Was the will burned along with the rest of Blackstone's library? Or was the will found and deliberately hidden or destroyed?

Sixty-one years later, Joseph Wilkinson, a former neighbor of John Blackstone, swore an affidavit [3] saying the younger Blackstone felt he had been cheated.

---

[3]   Preserved in the 1736/7 *Records Of Boundaries* in the Rhode Island Archives, Providence.

Providence

Joseph Wilkinson aged fifty-four years or thereabout Testifieth and Saith he was formerly acquainted with John Blackston dwelling near together and had often heard him say how he was wronged about his Fathers lands which his said Father Mr. William Blackston had formerly purchased of the Narraganset Sachems Connenicus and Meantenomy lying betwixt the Branches of Patuckett River where they were Settled and soon after his Fathers Death the Persons that was there look'd over his Fathers Papers and then he see his Fathers Deeds and could Read although Young and that he remembered well the marks of Connenicus & Meantomonys Bows & Arrows upon said Deeds after which time was not to be found; being not upon any Record and further saith not. Taken upon Engagement this Fourth Day of March Anno Domini 1736/7

Before me Wm Hopkins Justs Peace

Since the Indians left nothing unburned, John Stevenson inherited only land... no buildings, no books, no crops, no cattle.

Did Stevenson rebuild on this property? Probably. Did his stepbrother live with him? Probably not.

We do not know where young Blackstone lived during the years immediately following his father's death. Apparently, he did not "propose a man to the Court to be his guardian" as the June 1 court record stipulated. In October, the court appointed not one, but two men to be his guardians. The Old Colony records of Oct. 27, 1675 read:

Mr. Nathaniel Paine and Mr. Daniel Smith are appointed and approved by the court to be guardians unto John Blackstone the son of Mr. William Blackstone, deceased.

The Attleborough historian, Daggett, fills in a few details about John Stevenson's subsequent life:

Stevenson acquired a taste for solitary life by living with Blackstone, and resided here (It is believed alone) till his death. There is no evidence of his ever having been married. His time was devoted to the cultivation of his lands and the pleasures of hunting.

Twenty years after the death of his stepfather, John Stevenson died. The date was Sept. 16, 1695.

One of his brothers, James of Springfield, was appointed administrator of his estate. James' inventory, returned on Oct. 11, 1695, puts a value of L 57 5s 2d on John's entire estate. His house, lands and meadows were valued at L 50; his gun, cutlass and cartouch box, 10s etc.

It is interesting to note that, in the same legal record, John Stevenson's family name is spelled two ways - Stevenson and Stephenson - and that the term father-in-law was used to mean what we today call stepfather. In subsequent recordings of land, he is referred to as John Blackstone's brother rather than stepbrother.

This interchange of terms, as we have mentioned, even crept into the Massachusetts Historical Collection where Stevenson is called William Blackstone's son-in-law. It is no wonder the author of *Humours Of Utopia* found it easy to provide a daughter for the Rev. Mr. Blackstone.

****

Chapter Nine

JOHN BLACKSTONE, MINISTER'S SON, AND HIS FAMILY

Let us turn now to John Blackstone. How did the minister's son turn out?

Five months after the Rev. William Blackstone's death, Plymouth Colony put his 15-year-old orphaned son into the care of two permanent guardians. The Old Colony records of Oct. 27, 1675 read:

Mr. Nathaniel Paine and Mr. Daniel Smith are appointed and approved by the court to be guardians unto John Blackstone the son of Mr. William Blackstone, deceased.[1]

We read that John Blackstone did not live with his half brother, John Stevenson, after his father's death. Where, then, did he go? Did one of his guardians take him into his own household? Did his guardians apprentice him to a local cobbler, augmenting the tutelage his mother had already given him in working leather?

Possibly the teenage orphan was free enough and capable enough... or stubborn enough... to erect his own home on that portion of his father's land that was allotted to him. Mary Kent Davey Babcock, writing in *The Boston Transcript* of Sept. 24, 1930, says, "John Blackstone and his half brother, John Stevenson, lived side by side until 1692 when Blackstone, having squandered most of his inheritance, sold the rest to David Whipple of Providence..."

---

[1] *Old Colony Records* as quoted on pp. 68-69 of J. W. Blackstone's *Lineage And History Of William Blackstone*, 1907.

According to most early historians, John Blackstone was a "loose" young man, "a scapegrace and a prodigal." Bliss states he was "a fast young man who wasted his property in intemperance and idleness." [2]

Taking a more sympathetic view, Nathaniel Brewster Blackstone reminds us that John probably never experienced a true father-son relationship with his father, who was 65 years old when he was born. The Florida genealogist suspects, too, that John Blackstone did not get along with his half brother who was 16 years his senior. The fact that the two young men did not choose to live together seems to point to incompatibility.

There is also the possibility that cheating or maltreatment on the part of the Colony-appointed guardians soured young Blackstone's outlook on humanity in general.

John Blackstone's bad reputation was not confined to the neighborhood of Study Hill. Nine years after John became an orphan, the Town of Boston moved, via a deposition, to make sure John Blackstone, by then 23 years of age, would cause no trouble regarding the purchase of his father's Boston property, a transaction that had taken place 49 years before:

> ... lest some "pettifogger from Furnival's inn," like Morton, as Branford calls him, should put evil thoughts into John Blackstone's head; and to bar all possibility of disturbance from every quarter." [3]

Apparently, John Blackstone continued to live until 1689 on the banks of the river that today honors his father's name. He is mentioned in a 1682 deed referring to Ephraim Peirce whose land bordered the Blackstone land. His name was still on the Attleborough tax list in 1688. However, the following year, he figures as a non-resident proprietor. This may have been when he moved to Providence and took up the trade his mother had prepared him for: shoemaking and related leather work.

---

[2]   Bliss, *History Of Rehoboth*, p. 13

[3]   Deposition by John Odlin and others is in Mass. Hist. Coll., XIV, 202. Quoted by L. M. Sargent in 1849 in *Boston Evening Transcript*.

In 1690, John Blackstone, now 30 years of age, married Katherine Gorham in Providence. [4], [5]

The bride's brother, David Gorham of North Yarmouth, ME, invited the couple to move to Maine. Gorham pointed out that land costs up there in the north woods were reasonable and there were plenty of jobs to be had in the logging business. The newlyweds accepted both his advice and his hospitality.

They lived with the Gorhams, in their log house, until their first child was born in 1691. They named this son William, in honor of his grandfather. However, John Blackstone apparently did not find logging to his liking, and perhaps he did not like those long, cold Maine winters either. The couple decided to return to Blackstone's property on the banks of the Blackstone River.

In the spring, John and Katherine headed south, leaving Baby William with the Gorhams. His parents feared that the slow, rough journey would be too much for the infant.

After but a short time at the Study Hill farm, the couple moved to the town of Providence. It was in September 1692 that John sold his farm, then considered to be within the town of Rehoboth, to David Whipple.

DEED

To all to whom this deed of sale shall come, John Blaxton of Rehoboth in the Co. of Bristoll, formerly in the Colony of New Plymouth - but now of Mass. in New England, shoemaker, sendeth Greetg. for a valuable -- of this County in hand, and paid to him by David Whipple, husbandman, inhabitant of the town of Providence in the Narragansett Bay in New England, sells &c, his house and lands, (that is to say) his mansion house and --- on the east side of the River, called Pawtucket River, and lying and being within the precincts of Rehoboth aforesaid, 150 a. and is

---

[4] Nathaniel Brewster Blackstone, *The Life Of John Blackstone, 1660-1743, Only Son Of Rev. William Blackstone*, privately printed in Homestead, FL, 1974.

[5] Katherine is sometimes spelled Catharine. John Blackstone spelled his last name Blaxton.

situated on the Plaine c. d the West Plaine, b.d to the northward the land of Isaac Allen, to the southward the land of John Stephenson, to the w.d Pawtucket Rr. to the E. d part of it to the land of John Stephenson, and part of it to the highway, and part of it the Undivided land, with 20 a. allowed for a highway, &c. &c. the latter b.d Southward by a small run of water and 2 a.m. on the westirly side of the Country highway next the house.

Dated Sept. 10, 1692   Ack'd Oct. 26, 1692   John Blaxton
Witnessed by Tho. Oliver,   Before John Easton Gov.
     Anthony Sprague   By Wm. Carpenter Town Clerk
                              Rec'd Dec. 7, 1692 [6]

In her *Boston Transcript Article* mentioned previously, Babcock says that the "mansion house" and land described in this deed suggest "that in the ten years after his majority, he (John Blackstone) had acquired or retained a certain amount of capital."

Babcock uncovered another transaction that further indicates young Blackstone was no pauper. She writes:

Not a single biographer... has balanced this sale with one recorded on the same day, Sept. 10, 1692, wherein, "David Whipple of the towne of Providence husbandman in consideration of a valuable sum in current money of the country" conveys to "John Blackstone of ye town of Rehoboth, shoemaker, his mansion house and out houseing and land whereon the said house standeth and there unto adjoyneth it being 60 acres more or less." Other land conveyed brings the total acreage up to 110 acres, the property being Whipple's by inheritance from his father and by purchase from one of the original grantees of the Colony, John Steere. The deed bears also under date of Dec. 15, 1692, the release of Hannah, David Whipple's wife. Tho Olney in the capacity of "Town Clarke" signs the release and John Easton, the Governor, signs the acknowledgment of the deed on Oct. 26, 1692.

---

[6]   The original deed bearing John Blaxton's signature is in the possession of the Rhode Island Historical Society, a gift from John Whipple of Cumberland, RI.

Furthermore, on that same day, Sept. 10, 1692, John Blackstone assumed the role of gentleman farmer by leasing part of this property to John Daily of Providence. A year later, on Sept. 7, 1693, he sold the parcel to Daily.

That same year, 1693, according to Nathaniel Brewster Blackstone, John and Katherine took a boat to Boston to visit their son in North Yarmouth. They were delayed in Boston for a few days and were made welcome by an old friend of John's father, George Vaughan, a successful business man. Vaughan offered to set John Blackstone up in business in Portsmouth. Blackstone said he would think about it.

The couple found their son, now three years old, well and happy with the Gorhams and their children. They returned to Providence with him a few months later, Nathaniel Brewster Blackstone says. [7]

It was while they were in Maine that Blackstone's half brother, John Stevenson, died.

Two years later, on Nov. 21, 1695, Blackstone conveyed to James Phillipps "certain tracts and parcels of land which I purchased some time since of David Whipple." This was probably the portion he had retained when he first leased one half to Daily.

In the middle of 1696, John Blackstone became restless again. He went to Boston to see if Vaughan's offer still held. It did. Leaving his wife and child behind, Blackstone proceeded to open a cobbler's business in Portsmouth. Because of Vaughan's connections, his shop attracted a first-class clientele. He was soon doing well enough to send for Katherine and little William.

Nathaniel Brewster Blackstone says Katherine was unhappy about living in a strange neighborhood, so John made arrangements with Vaughan to have her and William take residence again in her brother's home in North Yarmouth. John visited them off and on until, early in 1698, he and his wife again returned to Providence. This time, seven-year-old William remained with the Gorham family.

---

[7]   Nathaniel Brewster Blackstone, *The Life Of John Blackstone, 1660-1743, Only Son Of Rev. William Blackstone*, privately printed in Homestead, FL, 1974.

The following year, 1699, John and Katherine Blackstone became parents a second time. They named this son John.

There is no record of this John's birth in Providence, but Samuel Greene Arnold explains the absence of such a record in the following manner: [8]

> The old Book of Records in the Archives of Providence show him (John Blackstone, the father) to be there in 1699. No birth of a child is recorded to him, but as many pages are missing, there might once have been such a fact recorded; and I establish the fact (of son John's date of birth) through the following facts: A child named John Blackstone was born that year, who after various voyagings about the world, finally became a man of character and property, and settled at Branford, CT, where he died, and the following is a copy from his tombstone. "In memory of John Blackstone, who departed this life Jan. 3, 1785, aged 85 years, eleven months, and 15 days." This tombstone, and the change in style, establishes his birth to be in 1699; and in a document still in existence, he states that he "was born in Providence, New England, in 1699." Now as there was then no other of that name in any of the New England colonies, I regard it as conclusive that this John, whose memorial is above copied, was the son of John Blackstone the shoemaker, and his wife Catherine (Gorham) of Providence; and grandson to the Pilgrim, many of whose nobler qualities he seemed to have inherited, instead of adopting the indolence of his father.

John and Katherine Blackstone and their second son seem to have remained in Providence for the next several years except for occasional visits to Maine to see the older son, William. [9]

---

[8] Samuel Greene Arnold, *History Of The State Of Rhode Island*, Vol. II, D. Appleton & Co., NY, 1860; Appendix O, p. 569.

[9] According to John Osborne Austin, John and Katherine Blackstone also had two daughters, but this is the only mention of daughters I have encountered. Page 22 of *The Genealogical Dictionary Of Rhode Island; Comprising Three Generations Of Settlers Who Came Before 1690* by John Osborne Austin, Baltimore: Genealogical Publishing Co., Inc., 1982.

Nathaniel Brewster Blackstone says that by 1713, John and Katherine started moving again... first to Attleborough, then to New Haven, and finally to Branford, CT, by 1714.

Here we run into a confusion of dates, some of them conflicting.

According to Daggett in his 1894 history, [10] the elder Blackstone couple continued to reside in Providence until 1718

> ... when he (the son of the Rev. William Blackstone) returned to Attleborough, and, with his wife, was legally warned out of town. For what cause does not appear, but may be conjectured. He had probably squandered his property, for tradition says he inherited but a small share of his father's prudence, and this was a precautionary measure on the part of the town against future liability for support - a customary proceeding in those days.

John Wilford Blackstone, writing in 1907, [11] put it this way, "He was banished from Attleborough in the year 1714 'as likely to become a public charge. Daggett's and J. W. Blackstone's dates differ by four years.

In 1720, another uncomplimentary reference to John Blackstone appears, this one in the Town Records of Providence:

> Att A Towne Councill held att Providence this 30th day of September 1720
> The Councill is Jn being Called by warrant This day Joseph Woodward being summoned appeared before the Councill to give an account of (bringing) John Blackstone and his wife into this Towne his answer was that Blackstones wife being not well his wife took her home out of piety being persuaded by som of the Neighbours on the other side of the River where Blackstone: (kept) and before they had ben with him a month: Cap Wilkinson told

---

10   John Daggett, *A Sketch Of The History Of Attleborough From Its Settlement To The Division*, Boston: Press of Samuel Usher, 1894, p. 75.

11   John Wilford Blackstone, *Lineage And History Of William Blackstone*, Frederic, WI: John Wilford Blackstone Jr., 1907.

him the said Woodward that If he Entertained Blackstone and his wife he ought to give bond for him: and the said Woodward Replyed that he would not

On the other hand, Nathaniel Brewster Blackstone says John Blackstone settled in Branford, CT, in 1714... six years before the above-mentioned item appeared in the Providence Town Records. [12]

In any case, Katherine Gorham Blackstone died in Branford in 1723. She was 53 and had been married to John Blackstone for 33 years.

If the life of John Blackstone is but dimly seen through insufficient facts, Katherine's is even more so. We see shadows of a wife who moved from city to city, sometimes living with her husband, sometimes living with her relatives. We see a woman eliciting such "piety" on the part of strangers for "being not well" that they take her and her husband into their home in spite of the frowns of the local town fathers. We see a mother whose first-born son was, for most of his childhood, brought up by her brother in far-away Maine.

John, her second son, too, was taken from her care, if one believes the records of the Attleborough Town Council. They state:

> Where as Richard Wicks of Attleborough came before this Councill and made his application before said Councill Concerning The Extreme Charge he has bin att in the nurssing of John Blackstone's child that was born in The Towne of Providence: - and after some debate had betweixt the Councill and the said Richard Wickes: and Likewise some Conferance had in Consideration of the premisses by the Towne Council betwixt themselves: -
> It is voted and ordered that the said Richard Wickes shall have the sum of ten pounds allowed him out of the Towne Treasury....bringing up said Child: upon the signing an Indenture for the bringing up and maintaining sd Childe untill he shall

[12]   Nathaniel Brewster Blackstone, *The Life Of John Blackstone, 1660-1743, Only Son Of Rev. WILLIAM BLACKSTONE*, Homestead, FL: 1974.

attaine to the age of twenty-one years: and then give him one new sute of apparil besides his other wareing Clothes and It is further voated and ordered that the overseers of the poore with two of The Justices of the peace for This Towne of Providence shall signe an Indenture of sd Child to the sd Richard Wickes his heirs Executors and administrators: but not to be assigned without the Consent of ye sd Councill or there successors.

The Childs name is John Blackstone Jun and he is to be Learned to Reade and to be brought up in the art of husbandrey.

The trouble with this piece of news is its date: Sept. 24, 1722. Young John, son of John and Katherine Blackstone, was 23 years old by then. Was Richard Wickes seeking retroactive reimbursement?

One wonders why the boy's father did not train him in his own trade, that of a cobbler. As it turned out, this young man did not remain a husbandman, either. He went to sea. In later property deeds of Branford, he is called John the Mariner.

After Katherine Blackstone died, the older John Blackstone sought the comfort of his friends, the Vaughans. George Vaughan was now dead, but his son, William Vaughan, made Blackstone as welcome as his father would have, and even set him up again in the shoemaking and repair business in Portsmouth, NH. This location put him close to his elder son, William, who by this time was living in Rochester, NH, with his wife, Abigail, and their children.

In 1731, old John Blackstone returned to Branford where his other son, John the Mariner, had established himself. Twelve years later, at age 83, he died.

No stone in the old Branford burial ground legibly marks the spot where the Rev. William Blackstone's only son is buried. However, one of John's 20th-century descendants who lives in that town, Paul Blackstone, points out, "A lot of those old brown stones are all chipped away leaving no indication as to whom they are for."

*****

Chapter 10

THE SAGE'S GRANDSONS

As we have seen, John and Katherine Blackstone had two sons: William, born in North Yarmouth, Maine, in 1691, and John, born in Providence, Rhode Island, eight years later. The childhood experiences of the two boys were utterly different. Not surprisingly, their adult lives were, too.

William, first grandson and namesake of the Sage of the Wilderness, was brought up for most part in his uncle David Gorham's household, a presumably more settled and sedate household than that of his parents. He must have felt more like a nephew than a son of John and Katherine Blackstone.

Nathaniel Brewster Blackstone [1] describes William's childhood years as "somewhat frustrating," noting that

> The first two and a half years of his life were with the Gorhams in Maine, the next two and a half in Providence with his parents. Then he went to Portsmouth for a spell, and back to North Yarmouth with his mother. In 1698, his parents again returned to Providence, leaving little William with the Gorhams once again. In the following year, his little brother, John, was born in Providence. From then on, William saw his parents only on occasional visits by them when they were able to make the trip up there.

The 20th-century genealogist goes on to say that young William was "far more blessed with his grandfather's traits of character and his ability to

---

[1] *The Life Of William Blackstone 1691-1779, First Son Of John And Katherine Blackstone,* a five-page pamphlet privately printed by the author, Homestead, FL, 1974.

learn, for example, how to get along in the wilderness; or with the Indians, keeping good health habits, and just plain living a good clean life, than he was of his own father's traits."

As he grew up, William learned about the lumbering business from his uncle and apparently made a good impression on three older men, Elisha Clark, the Dover-Portsmouth ferryman; a Sergeant John Hall of Dover; and Humphrey Varney, a Dover planter. Each of these men played an important role in his later life.

In 1713 or 1714, he married Abigail Varney Claridge, Humphrey Varney's daughter and widow of Ambrose Claridge of Portsmouth, NH. The bridegroom was 23. Abigail, who was born July 10, 1669, was 45 years of age. [2]

During the first four years of their marriage, Abigail presented her young husband with three daughters and a son: Patience born in 1715, Lydia in 1716, Susana in 1717 and William Jr. in 1718.

When William Blackstone married Abigail Varney Claridge, she already owned land in the Concheco region that her father had deeded to her and possibly some that her first husband left her. However, like his grandfather before him, Blackstone ran into land troubles. By 1719, a Richard Waldron brought suit against 12 of the Concheco settlers, finally dispossessing them all. [3]

The 12 included William Blackstone, planter, and his oldtime friend, Elisha Clark, ferryman, as well as Benjamin Mason, William Stiles, Howard Henderson, Peter Cook, Samuel Cosen, James Wilmet, Joseph Canney, John Foy, Samuel Alley and Richard Hammock.

Three years later, Blackstone, Richard Hammock and a James Hanson

---

[2]   According to Mary Kent Davey Babcock, a William Blackstone married Abigail Varney, granddaughter of Elder Starbuck, the Nantucket settler, before 1696 in Dover, NH. If this date were correct, William, the son of John and Katherine Blackstone, would have been only five years old at the time of his marriage.

[3]   Waldron was acting as administrator of his father's estate.

bought "one share betweixt them to be equally shared in the thirdly third share" in the first division of lots in the new town of Rochester. The town was incorporated May 10, 1722.

A couple of years later, about 1724, William had a dream. He dreamed of owning a big saw mill powered by a high waterfall. In his mind, he pictured a site where water running over a bed of solid rock might easily be dammed. He mentioned his dream to William Vaughan, his father's Portsmouth friend, and received that man's promise of financial backing and technical help when he was ready for them.

William found his dream spot near a small Maine harbor called Damariscotta by the Indians. By early spring, ready to begin work on his project, he set out for Damariscotta. He worked for 14 years before he was able to bring his family there to join him.

During this period, in 1730, his eldest daughter, Patience, married Josiah Clark, sixth-born child of Elisha Clark. The couple eventually had 10 children. In 1731, his second daughter, Lydia, married Samuel Hall, Sgt. John Hall's oldest son.

No doubt William journeyed the 100 miles or so from Damariscotta to attend his daughters' weddings. Perhaps he sailed. That would seem to have been easier. His father, too, was probably a wedding guest. This was during the time of the older man's final sojourn in the Portsmouth-Rochester area. Old John's second son, John, too, seems to have been living in the vicinity, because it was from Portsmouth harbor that, in 1728, the younger John went to sea.

While William was away, working in Damariscotta, his wife Abigail, along with Elisha Clark, Howard Henderson, James Wilmet and Joseph Canney complained to the Governor's Council about having had their Concheco land taken away from them. However, the complaint, dated April 4, 1729, was to no avail.

In 1738, having prepared a suitable dwelling, William set out to bring his family to Damariscotta to live with him. Abigail was now 69; Susana, 21; and William, Jr., 20. In 1743, the year William's father died in Branford, CT, Susana was married to James Hall, brother of her sister

Lydia's husband, Samuel Hall. William's three daughters and their husbands settled in the vicinity.

Vaughan and his engineer, Linscot, arrived in Damariscotta in 1741 and soon set up a sturdy dam and mill. In 1745, during the struggle between England and France over control of North America, Vaughan and Blackstone took time out to fight in the battle that destroyed Louisburg, the French fortress on Cape Breton Island. [4] Vaughan returned to England in 1746 and, much to William's sorrow, died at age 43.

William Blackstone was now 55. He was busy developing the Damariscotta Mill and establishing the town of Newcastle where he had built a very comfortable home. But again, there arose a dispute over the possession of land.

This time, it was the King's Agent, [5] Jonathan Jones, who claimed the Damariscotta land belonged to the king and that if William and his neighbors did not pay him taxes for it, he would confiscate it in the king's name.

William and his neighbors were driven out, just as his grandfather, the Rev. William Blackstone, had been. On Oct. 3, 1763, he vented his feelings in a deposition as follows:

> The deposition of William Blackstone of Newcastle, in the County of Lincoln, and of lawful age, testifies and says, that I have lived at Damariscotta Saw Mills for about 26 years and improved with others who worked at said Mills, all the land and meadows on bothe sides of said river, and fresh pond to the nor'ward thereof under William Vaughan, Esq., deceased, and since his death, myself with sundry others have held and improved said lands and meadows for about 13 years under James Noble, Esq., except what lots of land on said side of river and pond, Noble sold to any persons, and have ever since improved said land and meadows under said Noble, the whole length of said pond on the

---

[4]   Amory says "One of John Blackstone's sons with the rank of lieutenant lost his life in Louisburg," but adds that the statement has not been verified.

[5]   Agent for George II to 1760 and then for George III.

West side of said pond, about half way to the Sheepscott River and pond, and never was disturbed in possession by any claimer whatsoever, 'till June last, 1763, when one Jonathan Cook, Jonathan Jones, John Jones and Anthony Chapman, have with a great number of men, although forbid, as I have heard, entered on the premises, which was held under said Noble, and built a saw mill, fenced in a large tract of land possest under Noble, as aforesaid and gives out that they will hold the same by a strong hand, as I have heard. The deponent further testifies that he with others paid the yearly rent for the above described and premises to the above named Vaughan and Noble, during the above mentioned term and further saith not.

Dated at New Castle, Oct. 3, 1763
William Blackstone

William died in his home across the bay near the Bristol-Nobleboro town lines.

When William's brother, John, went to sea in 1728, he was 29 and had been married a year to Elizabeth Foot. [6], [7]. "Soon after 1700," he established his home in Branford, CT. There, he was known as John the Mariner.

John Blackstone, the mariner, bought considerable land in Branford and, to this day, a portion of the town overlooking Long Island Sound is called Blackstoneville.

On First Avenue, Branford, there stands a big old red house that once commanded a view of the sound. Today, many other houses stand in the way. This is known as the John Blackstone House.[8]

Since the main part of the house was built in or about 1680 and John the

---

[6]   Sometimes spelled Foote.

[7]   They were wed April 2, 1727.

[8]   Around 1890, the house was bought by Winfred H. Hotchkiss. He developed the area around the house as a shore resort that became known as Hotchkiss Grove.

Mariner did not arrive in Branford until "soon after 1700," he was obviously not its builder. He and his descendants lived in it long enough, however, to have the Blackstone name attached to it. An ell was added later.

The house seems to have originally belonged to the Foot family, probably his wife Elizabeth's family.

A July 31, 1732 document states that Caleb Pamerley Jr of Branford sold to "John Blakiston Marriner" for 30 pounds "one acre of fifth division land near Indian Rock... laid out to me in right of my former wife Elisabeth Dec'd unto ye estate of Robert Foot dec'd.

In an entry relating to a C. A. Blackstone, the *New Haven County, Connecticut, Commemorative Biographical Record* [9] mentions that "Soon after 1700, a John Blackstone appeared in Branford... a mariner from Rhode Island with his wife Rebecca. He was probably the grandson of the Rev. William Blackstone."

It seems strange that John's second wife, Rebecca Harrison, is the one named as arriving with him, since his first wife, Elizabeth Foot, did not die until April 2, 1727. The exact date of John's second marriage is not known but it must have been after 1727. Apparently, in this case, the term "Soon after 1700" was used loosely.

Rebecca was born in 1705 and died 60 years later, Oct. 8, 1765.

Eleven years later, at age 77, John the Mariner wed Sarah Huggins. Her birth and death dates are unknown but we know she was John's wife for eight years. According to a marker in the Branford burial ground, John the Mariner died on Jan. 3, 1785 at age 85.

Grave of "John the Mariner" in Branford, CT Cemetery.

*****

9   Published in Chicago in 1902.

Chapter 11

𝕿𝕳𝕰 𝕳𝕴𝕷𝕷 𝕿𝕳𝕬𝕿 𝕯𝕴𝕾𝕬𝕻𝕻𝕰𝕬𝕽𝕰𝕯

During his half century of residence in America, the Rev. William Blackstone moved but twice... from Wessagusset to Shawmut; then from Shawmut to Study Hill. He lived on Study Hill for 40 years and was buried there.

Any visitor to the Lonsdale section of Cumberland should easily find Study Hill. Several old writers described it in great detail. Yet, no hill fitting their descriptions exists! The secret location of the hill, for many years, was buried in a few obscure records. [1]

Here is how, in 1894, John Daggett portrayed Study Hill in his Attleborough history: [2]

> The place which he chose for his residence was a truly beautiful and romantic spot, such as a recluse and a lover of nature would select. The place where his house stood was a small hill the surface of which would make an acre or more; on the east was a gradual ascent, but on the west it rose abruptly from the river to a height of sixty or seventy feet; there the Blackstone wound gracefully at its base, forming a slight curve at a short distance south of the hill, but the river has since then enlarged its channel at this place, and it finally washed the very base of the hill, as if attracted to the spot by a grateful remembrance of him who first sought its banks and loved its stream and whose honored name it now bears.

---

[1]   Blackstone's bones, however, have had at least three resting places. Today, no one knows where they are.

[2]   John Daggett, *A Sketch Of The History Of Attleborough From Its Settlement To The Division*, Boston: Press of Samuel Usher, 1894.

The summit of the hill commanded a fine view of the "valley of the Blackstone," to a distance of more than a mile on the south. On the east was a delightful and fertile valley consisting of a few acres which opened to the south on the borders of the meadow, and was bounded on the east and northeast by a gentle eminence, on the top of which ran the "Mendon road," so often mentioned in the ancient land records. This valley was cultivated by the hands of Blackstone; here was his orchard, where the author (Daggett) has seen the stumps of apple trees, cut down within his remembrance, which were said to have grown from the sprouts of the first trees planted by the hermit. His well, too, was long pointed out at the southern border of this valley and long after it was filled up with moss and weeds the pure water still bubbled up from its fountains. His grave was also designated, though with less certainty, in the orchard, about two rods east from the foot of the hill and north of the well. The "flat stone which it is said marked his grave," finally became invisible, either from removal or from being buried under the surface.

John Wilford Blackstone repeated the same details 13 years later, adding: [3]

After his death, and after many years, the spot on which he lived returned to a state of nature. Heavy timber grew on "Study Hill," and less than one hundred years ago, its surface was covered with a thrifty growth of young trees. Oaks of a hundred years had been cut from the "Hill."

Earlier in his book, John Wilford Blackstone informs his readers: [4]

His dwelling which he called "Study Hall," was a few rods from the bank of the river near the hill which ascended by a gentle slope and his orchard was just east of the hill. This he called "Study Hill" a name it long retained. The place is about three

---

[3]   John Wilford Blackstone, *Lineage And History Of William Blackstone*, Frederic, WI: John Wkilford Blackstone Jr., 1907.

[4]   Ibid. pp. 45-46

miles above Pawtucket in the present town of Lonsdale, where the late Simon Whipple resided. The Indian name of the place was "Waurvepoonseag" - the place of snares or nets - "Waurvee" meaning a goose. This name is mentioned in the Plymouth records in describing the boundary of the North Purchase in 1661. "From Rehoboth, ranging upon the Pawtucket River to a place where our Blackstone now sojourneth called by the natives, "Waurvepoonseag."

No traces remain today of the cellar hole, the well, the grave markers... or even his beloved hill!

And for good reason. Study Hill was carted away in the 1880's to make a level site for the Ann and Hope Mill, one of the tremendous new textile factories of the Lonsdale Company. William Blackstone's Study Hill had to make way for industrial progress...for the birth of the Industrial Revolution in America.

The obituary of one John Cullen, an Irish immigrant who became the area's leading excavator, teamster, cattle trader etc, describes this major earth-moving project : [5]

The Ann and Hope Mill as viewed on a post card published around 1900

---

[5] John Cullen died Jan. 14, 1908 at his home in Limerock and was buried in St. Joseph's Cemetery, Mendon Road, Ashton, after a big funeral in St. Joseph's Church.

In 1886, when the Lonsdale Company decided to build the Ann and Hope mill, Mr. Cullen was awarded the contract for the excavating work. This was the most important work of the kind in which he had engaged and he carried it out with his usual energy. The work involved making a complete change in the field in which the mill was placed, clearing away the elevation known as "Study Hill," which tradition said was the favorite haunt of William Blackstone, the first white settler in Rhode Island, whose remains rested in the same field.

Note well that the obituary writer describes Study Hill as Blackstone's "favorite haunt." He does not say the house was there. Perhaps the Whipple family was more accurate when it positioned the Blackstone residence farther east, basing this assumption on what was pointed out to them by the Honorable Judge Dexter.

L. M. Sargent added more credence to this theory when, in 1849, he wrote in the Boston *Evening Transcript*: [6]

> ... for the ascent of the hill or knoll, as it is sometimes called, is so steep, that to have procured wood or water, or water alone, would have been next to impossible.   Besides <u>reducio ad absurdum</u>, the Whipple family, in whose possession the land has ever remained since it was sold to them by Blackstone's son, John Blackstone, says that the house was in the meadow, east side of the hill. And the Hon. Judge Dexter of Cumberland, who resides near the spot, tells me that, within his recollection, Blackstone's cellar, with the stoning was plainly to be seen; and pointed out to me the spot, about four rods east of the hill, and two east from his grave. His well, with the stoning almost entire, is still to be seen, a few rods south of the cellar and grave, on the second table and meadow.

Was the Blackstone house east of the crest of the hill, and the grave on the west side, nearer the river?

---

6   L. M. Sargent over the signature of "Saveall, *The Blackstone Family: Being Sketches, Biographical And Genealogical, Of William Blackstone,* published in 1849 in the *Evening Transcript,* Boston and republished in 1857 in Norwich, CT, by Lorenzo Blackstone of Norwich, CT, "for the gratification of the family circle."

In a letter to David W. Balfour, a member of the Cumberland Historic District Commission, dated Oct. 30, 1980, John H. Meharg, a Cumberland resident, wrote the following:

> ... My mother told me that when she came to Lonsdale in 1885, where the Ann and Hope is, there was a wooded slope ending near the railroad tracks and in the summer, the folks in the area would assemble there to chat. In this area, she said, there was a small white stone which marked what was said to be Blackstone's grave.
>
> The entire slope was removed to make room for the Ann and Hope Mill. Also, the present Ann and Hope group have further cut into the land on the Broad Street side in the rear of the mill to make additional parking space. Furthermore, the slope to the south of the steps from Broad Street has been removed for a similar reason.
>
> It appears to me that the portion of High Street between Blackstone St. and Dexter St. originally sloped to the river. I am inclined to believe in Blackstone's day, the river was further to the East and that, when the railroad was laid out, a good deal of the river was filled in, thus creating the steep banks that you can observe if you cut across the tracks in front of the Ann and Hope.
>
> If the above assumption is correct, Blackstone's home would in all likelihood have been somewhere in front of the Ann and Hope, as he would want to be near the water to secure the same for household purposes as well as to have the use of the same for his animals.

Meharg puts Study Hall near the river because he feels Blackstone would have needed water "for household purposes" and "for his animals." This water would have been only to supplement his well, however. Several witnesses mention having seen Blackstone's well. Meharg's statements about the changes in the course of the river and the filling in to provide a bed for the railroad tracks as well as the cutting into the hill to expand the parking grounds are all quite plausible when one observes the terrain as it exists today.

Perhaps the most accurate record we have of Study Hall's exact location is a map drawn by the Rev. Ezra Stiles, early president of Yale University, after he visited William Blackstone's grave in 1771. President Stiles is said to have left "a careful map of the whole region, marking the homes of Blackstone, Roger Williams and Samuel Gorton, the Patriarchs of New England history..."

Having established that Study Hill and Blackstone's grave have been replaced by the Ann and Hope mill building, the question still remains, "Where are William Blackstone's bones today?"

*****

Chapter 12

WILLIAM BLACKSTONE'S GRAVE

If William Blackstone's original resting place was usurped by an industrial structure, where are his remains today?

Daggett gives this account of the first exhumation and of the beginning of an organization whose sole purpose was to erect an appropriate monument over the final resting place of the "sage of the wilderness:" [1]

> On the one hundred and eightieth anniversary of his death, (1855) an effort was made to arouse public interest in the raising of funds to erect a suitable monument to William Blackstone. A few weeks later, on July 4, 1855, the anniversary of his marriage, quite a number of people gathered at his grave. The spot was then "designated by two small boulders of semi-crystalized quartz rock." An association was formed called the "Blackstone Monument Association." Officers were elected and a constitution adopted. Any persons, without regard to "age, sex, sect or color," by presenting their names and subscribing ten cents, were thereby made members of the association. Appropriate exercises were held; and an oration was delivered by Mr. S. C. Newman, a lineal descendent of the first minister of Rehoboth. This was followed by the singing of an ode, and impromptu speeches.

Although considerable enthusiasm was manifested, nothing in the way of a monument was constructed. One wonders who kept the dimes that were collected that day. For many years thereafter, Blackstone's grave was neglected and its site unknown to most people.

---

[1] *A Sketch Of The History Of Attleborough From Its Settlement To The Division* by John Daggett, edited and completed by his daughter, Amelia Daggett Sheffield, Boston: Press of Samuel Usher, 1894.

BLACKSTONE
MONUMENT.

PUBLIC NOTICE.
JULY 4TH, 1856.

The members of the "BLACKSTONE MONUMENT ASSOCIATION," and all other Ladies and Gentlemen so disposed, are hereby notified and invited to assemble at the celebrated "CATHOLIC OAK," on the original homestead of the venerated Blackstone, near the Lonsdale Depot, on July 4th, at 10 o'clk., a.m.

☞ Suitable and appropriate exercises may be expected.

A beautiful model of the proposed Mausoleum in honor of CIVIL AND RELIGIOUS LIBERTY will be exhibited; the

GREAT RECORD BOOK!

of the Association, exceeding in size and style all the books of the age, will be open to public inspection and for the reception of members. This is the first Anniversary of an Association which one year ago commenced with a single member and now numbers its members by thousands, and is destined to be the largest Association in the World.

☞ Refreshments will be provided, and Excursion Trains will run to and from the place.

BY ORDER OF THE PRESIDENT.

A. CRAWFORD GREENE & BROTHERS, PRINTERS, Prov.

S. C. NEWMAN, Sec'y.

Then came the Lonsdale Company and its plans to build the Ann and Hope Mill. Company records include the following entries:

Special Meeting, April 28, 1886

Reference having been made to a tradition that William Blackstone the earliest English settler in the present State of Rhode Island was buried beneath the site selected for the new mill, it was VOTED that the Agents be authorized and requested to ascertain so far as possible the identity of the grave and to remove the remains, if any are found, to another spot for burial with a suitable memorial stone.

VOTED that the Agents be requested to consult Mr. Lorenzo Blackstone as to the identity of the grave and to invite him to be present when the remains are removed.

Special Meeting, July 26, 1886

The Agents reported that on the sixth day of May, the grave of William Blackstone was opened by Messrs. Miles & Luther, well-known Undertakers from Providence, and that the human remains found therein consisted of a few small pieces of bone and a quantity of pulverized bone resembling lime dust, and that with these were also found a number of nails of ancient make such as might have been used in a coffin long ago. All these were carefully gathered and are now kept in charge of the Superintendent for burial at a future time.

By the invitation of the Agents, the opening of the grave and the exhumation of its contents were witnessed by Mr. Lorenzo Blackstone of Norwich, Conn., and by Mr. William Gammell, President of the Rhode Island Historical Society.

Annual Meeting, February 6, 1889

Upon Motion of Mr. William Gammell, it was VOTED that the Agents be authorized and instructed to erect a monument to the memory of the Rev. William Blackstone, the first white settler in Rhode Island, who dwelt and died upon the spot now occupied by the Ann and Hope Mill, this monument to be placed in front of the Mill and near the place of his interment. [2]

---

[2] William Gammell, in addition to being president of the Rhode Island Historical Society, was on the board of directors of the Lonsdale Company.

Special Meeting, July 24, 1889
 Whereas since the Annual Meeting of the Company, the descendants of Rev. William Blackstone, through their representative, Mr. W. N. Blackstone, have expressed an earnest desire to bear the expense of erecting the monument to his memory, it is VOTED that the Blackstone family be allowed to defray the expense of the monument which had been ordered by the Agents. The inscriptions upon the three faces are to remain the same; but on the fourth face will recite that this monument is "Erected by the lineal descendants of William Blackstone" and such portions of the previous votes of the Company as are inconsistent therewith are hereby rescinded.

Special Meeting, October 17, 1889
 The Agents reported that the Blackstone monument was completed and that the entire expense had been defrayed by the Blackstone family.

For another account of the removal of William Blackstone's bones and the erection of his monument, we turn again to the Attleborough historian, John Daggett, and to his daughter, Amelia Daggett Sheffield, who edited her father's notes and brought them up to date:

 While this work of demolition was going on, the bones of Mr. Blackstone were disinterred in the presence of Mr. Lorenzo Blackstone of Norwich, Conn., and of President Gammell of the Rhode Island Historical Society. These were placed in an appropriate box and again buried under the building, in which there will be a monument to his name...
 ...When the grave of Mr. Blackstone was discovered, "fragments of a coffin and hammered nails such as were made in those days, and pieces of bones were found," and "the sides of the grave were plainly visible." It was a "solitary grave," no indications of any other being visible, and it would seem that Blackstone must have buried his wife elsewhere. That the grave found was that of William Blackstone there can be no reasonable doubt, since now long ancient tradition has always pointed to that vicinity as his burial place.

Earlier in his book, Daggett wrote that "one Alexander, who was drowned in the river, was buried, it is said, by the side of Mr. Blackstone." He added this logical question, "Is it not probable that his wife was also buried at the same place?"

Daggett noted that this Alexander was "supposed to be the Thomas Alexander mentioned by Savage in GEN. DICT., vol. 1, p. 26, as son of Nathaniel. How he came here, and why, is unknown."

The finding of the solitary grave leaves us no clue as to where either Sarah Fisher Stevenson Blackstone or Thomas Alexander is buried.

A third version of the exhumation was printed in *The Pawtucket Gazette:*

On Thursday afternoon of last week, the grave was quietly opened by employees of Miles & Luther, the Providence undertakers, in the presence of a small company of gentlemen.

After removing about four feet of earth, indications of sepulture were apparent. First, one nail, very rusty, was found, then another and still another, until quite a number of them were collected.

Beside the nails, quite a number of bones were exhumed... The length of the coffin in which Blackstone was placed more than two centuries ago was manifest by the distance of the nails found at each end of the grave, and also the manner in which the bones lay, that is, lengthwise with the head and foot of the grave.

Marcia Green, writing in *The Evening Times,* Pawtucket, March 5, 1985, notes that the bones and nails were entrusted to Lonsdale Company Superintendent G. W. Pratt to keep until the mill would be completed and a monument erected.

Amelia Daggett Sheffield [3] describes the subsequently-built monument this way:

The monument stands a very few yards from the grave and in a line with it. The precise spot (of the original grave) is covered by Lonsdale Co's Ann and Hope Mill. The monument was erected by some of the descendants of William Blackstone, and the inscription was written by a member of the Lonsdale Co.

---

[3]   The tower on the oldest part of the mill carries the date 1886. The Daggett book was published in 1894.

It is of granite about twelve feet high, - the base five or six feet square and the shaft a foot or more smaller, tapering slightly. It is within the enclosed grounds of the mill, surrounded by the vivid green of a beautiful green lawn, the only object on it.

On the front face of the monument, beneath a cross carved in the stone, viewers read these words: "The grave of the Reverend William Blackstone, founder of the town of Boston, and the first white settler in Rhode Island." On the left side, is written: "Coming from Boston to this spot in 1635, he died May 26, 1675, aged over eighty years and was here buried." On the right face is: "A student of Emmanuel College, Cambridge, he took holy orders in the Church of England, in whose communion he lived and died." The rear panel reads: "Erected by the lineal descendants of William Blackstone A.D. 1889."

For many years, the bones of William Blackstone and a few rusty nails lay beneath this monument, in the metal-covered box in which Superintendent Pratt had placed them.

Commenting on the placement of Blackstone's monument in such an industrial environment, John Wilford Blackstone wrote in his 1907 booklet:

The sculptured shaft rears itself not amid the giant trees beside his flowing river, but near the giant engine by whose mighty power the hum of whirring spindles is heard unceasingly. The spirit of the gentle sage could scarcely reconcile itself to such a change, and must have passed saddened away from its accustomed haunts forever.

The late John H. Meharg, in his 1980 letter to David Balfour quoted previously, describes the setting thusly:

The A & H mill originally comprised the four-story section. The two-story unit was added later.

In the period of textile prosperity, the front of the mill (that facing the river) and part of the northern and southern portions were encased by a high iron fence -about seven feet tall. Between the fence and the mill building - a distance of about 100 feet - there was a lawn with a walk. The Blackstone monument was located a short distance west of the mill building near where the two-story and four-story adjoined. There was also a wide walk to the outside of the fence fronting the mill with an iron pipe fence - about waist-high - on the further side of which was a stretch of grass with a row of trees.

One had to get permission at the mill office to get close enough to the monument to read its inscriptions.

The remains of William Blackstone rested in this lawn-covered plot, undisturbed except by noise, from 1889 until the early 1940's. At that time, the vast New England textile industry was lured by the promise of cheaper help to move to the South. Like so many other factory buildings, the Ann and Hope became an empty shell.

Then came World War II. The United States Navy transformed the Ann and Hope building into a repair depot for heavy equipment. The fence and the lawn gave way to the accoutrements of war. A spur track from the railroad ran to the building. Blackstone's monument stood ignored and in danger of being damaged amid the turmoil.

Meharg was a member of the First Presbyterian Church, then located at the corner of Broad and Cumberland Streets, overlooking the Ann and Hope complex. [4] He suggested to church officials that the monument be moved to a small plot of church property on the opposite side of Broad Street. In his previously quoted letter to David Balfour, he wrote:

> After some very agreeable negotiations between the then owner of the property and the Navy Department, the monument was moved to its present location in 1944.
> I do not know whether Blackstone's remains were removed at the same time. Neither do I know if they were buried near or under the monument when it was erected in the mill yard. The minutes of the Lonsdale Company do not seem to be clear on this point. [5]

---

[4]   The church building was subsequently sold to Marques Wood Crafts, a home renovation company, and a new church, Calvin Presbyterian Chburch, was built on Angell Road, Cumberland.

[5]   Mehard's letter to Balfour adds this item: "Incidentally, there is a road in front of the A & H known as Study Hill Road. Just how far west from the mill property it begins, I do not know, but it is there any time the town wants to utilize it."

Marcia Green's *Evening Times* article mentions that the negotiations for the transfer of the monument were made between a navy chaplain and Meharg's minister.

Standing by the monument to the Rev. William Blackstone in Cumberland are Mr. and Mrs Paul Blackstone and their son John, of Branford, CT.

Since then, the Town of Cumberland has maintained the tiny park around William Blackstone's monument. It is situated close to the Broad Street sidewalk that overlooks the rear parking lot of what is today the Ann and Hope Discount Store. [6]

The late Robert E. Furey of El Cerrito, CA, remembered seeing the box containing William Blackstone's remains. His father, the late James Furey, was the building's plant engineer from 1943, when the Navy was using it, through the time it was owned by a realty company that preceded the Ann and Hope Discount Store. The elder Furey died in January 1965 and his son passed away in August of 1992.

The younger Furey, was an electronic engineer, used to work for his

---

[6]   Said to be the first discount store in the United States.

father during school vacations. In a telephone conversation with this author March 14, 1990, he brought the story of the missing bones up to the 1960's:

> It seems to me the box of William Blackstone's bones was dug up after World War II. The realty company bought the building from the Navy and was renting it out to several different kinds of businesses. It was constructing a separate cottage to be used as an office for the Almadon Co., a weaving business owned by a mother and her two sons. They found it too noisy to have an office in their weave shed.
>
> While digging to extend utilities to that cottage, a backhoe or shovel ran into a box. It was a wooden box sealed in lead... heavy lead foil. Its corners were soldered. It was about 12x12x16 inches in size. Inside, were a lot of handmade nails and a few fragments of bones. The shovel or backhoe damaged it a bit. It was opened because no one knew what it was at first.
>
> The box had been buried just north of the north tower, the tower closest to Mill Street. It had been dug up by 1949.
>
> The box sat for many years in the storeroom behind my father's office. His office was downstairs on the back of the building, the side nearest Broad Street.
>
> It seems to me that, in the 1960's, when Ann and Hope was expanding, they moved my father's office. I'm not sure what happened to the box. My mother and I wanted my father to offer the box to the Rhode Island Historical Society or some one like that, but he didn't get around to it. [7]

So, we are left with the big question: Where is that lead-covered box, the second coffin of the Rev. William Blackstone?

Unrecognized, was it thrown out when the building was being remodelled to serve as a department store? The truth is, we do not know.

*****

---

[7] Furey further reports that the cottage was demolished shortly before his father died in January 1965.

Chapter 13

𝔚𝔥𝔬 𝔚𝔞𝔰 𝔚𝔦𝔩𝔩𝔦𝔞𝔪 𝔅𝔩𝔞𝔠𝔨𝔰𝔱𝔬𝔫𝔢 ... 𝔯𝔢𝔞𝔩𝔩𝔶?

Was the Rev. William Blackstone "a mover and a shaker"? Was he a sage? Did he influence history? Or will he remain a romantic figure, shrouded forever in mystery?

Blackstone elicits exalted praise from some; dismissal as a "footnote in history" from others. What was he really like?

John Wilford Blackstone, writing in 1907, acclaimed his ancestor:

> The unprejudiced verdict now is, that the muse of history shows upon her tablets no figure more unique, elusive and romantic, no mind more profound, vigorous and virile, no soul more pure and exalted and no prescience more far reaching among all Americans of his time, than is shown in the record of the hermit sage of Study Hill. [1]

As a descendant, John Wilford Blackstone may have had some difficulty in recognizing an "unprejudiced verdict." But others, not of the Blackstone clan, have heaped the Rev. William Blackstone with sundry qualities, too.

"Blackstone was no ordinary man," claims the Rev. B. F. DeCosta. [2] He adds,

---

[1]   *Lineage And History Of William Blackstone* by John Wilford Blackstone of Minneapolis, Minn., published in 1907 by John Wilford Blackstone Jr., Frederic, Wis.

[2]   *William Blackstone In His Relation To Massachusetts And Rhode Island* by Rev. B. F. DeCosta, articles that appeared Sept. 25 and Oct. 2, 1880 in *The Churchman*.

The glimpses that we have of his character prove that he possessed qualifications which, under other circumstances, might have made him one of the foremost men of New England. His motto was "Toleration;" the thought being held in a lofty sense that never dawned upon the vision of Roger Williams. He appears every way superior to the times, and stands like some tall rock in the sea whose summit is bathed in untroubled light, while tumultuous waves beat below. At a later period he would have been the friend and collaborator of Berkeley, and together they might have pursued the paths of contemplative philosophy, and labored to lay foundations for education and the Church. [3]

Conrad Aiken's encominium is one of the most colorful. In the foreword to his long poem about Blackstone called *The Kid*, Aiken wrote:

He (Blackstone) is a tantalizing figure, in many respects the true prototypical American; ancestor alike of those pioneers who sought freedom and privacy in the "wide open spaces," or the physical conquest of an untamed continent; and those others, early and late, who struggle for it in the darker kingdom of the soul. Daniel Boone and Johnny Appleseed were his grandchildren. But so, too, were Thoreau and Melville and Henry Adams. And the outlaws, the lone wolves, the lost souls - yes, these as well.

The unknown author of *Famous Men In Rhode Island* concedes to Blackstone "undisputed place in history as the State's first white landholder," but discounts any further importance by saying, "William Blackstone had no great influence on the social, commercial or political growth of Rhode Island."

John W. Haley, author of a series of Rhode Island history books published in 1939, beams a slightly more flattering light on Blackstone. He gives him credit, at least, for being a persistent man of principle: [4]

---

[3] The Irish-Anglican theologian and philosopher, Bishop George Berkeley 1685-1753, eventually settled in Middletown, RI, in a home he called "Whitehall."

[4] *The Old Stone Bank History Of Rhode Island* by John W. Haley, Vol. III, p. 18. No city; no publisher indicated. 1939.

In no way can he be classed as a great leader in man's age-long struggle to gain true liberty and freedom of conscience, but he was one who wanted such privileges and he persisted in his endeavors until his ideals had been attained to their fullest degree. It seems proper that William Blackstone found absolute independence of the individual man in things of the spirit in lands that are today a part of Rhode Island, the acknowledged birthplace of full and complete religious liberty.

Blackstone's independent spirit draws a brisker salute from Andrew Duehring in an article that appeared June 24, 1963 in *The Providence Journal:*

Many historians have minimized the pioneer clergyman's contributions to history - a name for a river, a few apple trees... But he was something more than a mere contributor of history.
He was an independent man.

Blackstone's integrity is rated higher than that of his contemporary New Englanders by James C. Byrne, late president of the Woonsocket (RI) Historical Society. In a paper read before the society June 22, 1964 and reported in *The Woonsocket Call* of June 23, Byrne described Blackstone as "one of the real pioneers of New England, a learned and a truly religious man, which is more than can be said of many of our early settlers."

From the perspective of one who had delved deeply into William Blackstone's life, Nathaniel Brewster Blackstone warned that very little can be found to prove his subject's alleged lofty thoughts and opinions. In the Epilogue of his 1974, 20-page, privately-printed booklet about the "sage of the wilderness," the author says:

Not a little has since been said and written of Blackstone to the effect that he was "a memorable man," that he was centuries in advance of the age in which he lived, that his motto was "Toleration," and he possessed qualifications which, under other circumstances, might have made him one of the foremost men of New England. This may, or may not be so, but the simple fact is that we have no means of forming any definite judgment about his opinion or intellectual power.

He was a singular man and as is apt to be the case with singular men when dead, he excites our curiosity. The graduate of a university, he crossed the ocean almost immediately after taking his degree, and he carried with him into the wilderness his books and his studious habits. He then chanced to make his home on the site of a future great city, where he lived the life of a devout recluse - almost a hermit. He disliked restraint and society, but there is no reason whatever to suppose that he had a peculiarly active or vigorous mind. If he was gifted that way, he succeeded most effectually in hiding his gift from the world.

Robert Shackleton [5] takes a much more romantic view of William Blackstone:

What an interesting life story Blaxton's must have been! How it tantalizes the imagination!   And yet, as to so much of the romantic in New England, the New England mind is rather cold toward him.

Shackleton felt that this coldness was strikingly illustrated "by no less a man than Henry Cabot Lodge who, after telling of the mystery of Blaxton and of the little that was ever known of him, remarked that... 'although all this seems dimly mysterious and excites curiosity, the story would 'no doubt prove commonplace enough' if we could know more about it!"

What surprised Shackleton was that Lodge came to this conclusion even after admitting that Blackstone was "a Cambridge man who exiled himself, with his library, to the absolutely unbroken wilderness and marvelously made a charming home here, with his flowers and books..."

The diverse judgements of these observers leave us with the question, "Just exactly who WAS the Rev. William Blackstone?"

This biography is not a finished portrait. It may be likened, instead, to an artist's rough sketch. I have used all the material I could find, but I suspect there is much more out there.

---

[5]   *The Book Of Boston*, Robert Shackleton, Philadelphia: Penn Publishing Co., 1923.

I invite all who delve in early New England history, as they pursue their studies, to watch for bits and pieces about William Blackstone and send them... no matter how trivial... to

THE DEPOSITORY OF BLACKSTONE HISTORY
Blackstone Valley Tourism Council
P.O. Box 7663
Cumberland, RI 02864

Some day, when all the pieces are in, William Blackstone will step forward... whole and complete.

*****

NEW ENGLAND

BLACKSTONE RIVER VALLEY NATIONAL HERITAGE CORRIDOR

BIBLIOGRAPHY

Aiken, Conrad, *The Kid,* Edinburgh: R&R Clark, Ltd., first published in 1947 by John Lehman, Ltd. in Great Britain.

Amory, Thomas Coffin, Paper presented before The Boston Society, Boston, Nov. 9, 1880.

Arnold, Samuel Greene, *History of the State of Rhode Island,* New York, D. Appleton & Co., 1860. Vol. II.

Austin, John Osborne, *Genealogical Dictionary of Rhode Island, Comprising Three Generations of Settlers Who Came Before 1690,* Baltimore: Genealogical Publishing Co., Inc., 1982.

Babcock, Mary Kent Davey, *The Boston Transcript,* Sept. 24, 1930.

Bayles, Richard M., *History of the State of Rhode Island and Providence Plantations, Providence, 1920.* Vol. I.

Bicknell, Thomas W, *History Of The State Of Rhode Island And Providence Plantations,* Providence, Vol. I, 1920.

Blackiston, Patrick, Paper published in England about 1975.

Blackstone, John Wilford, *Lineage and History of William Blackstone,* Frederic, WI: Privately printed by John Wilford Blackstone Jr., 1907.

Blackstone, Lorenzo (See Sargent.)

Blackstone, Nathaniel Brewster, *The Biography of the Rev. William Blackstone & His Ancestors & Descendants,* Privately printed in Homestead, FL: 1974.

Blackstone, Nathaniel Brewster, *The Blackstone Family, Being Sketches,* Privately printed in Homestead, FL: 1974.

Blackstone, Nathaniel Brewster, *The Life of John Blackstone, 1660-1743, Only Son of Rev. William Blackstone*, Privately printed in Homestead, FL: 1974.

Blackstone, Nathaniel Brewster, *The Life of William Blackstone 1691-1779, First Son of John and Katherine Blackstone*, Privately printed in Homestead, FL: 1974.

Blackstone, Nathaniel Brewster, *Origin of the Name, Coat of Arms, Crest*, Privately printed in Homestead, FL: 1974.

Bliss, Leonard Jr., *History of Rehoboth*, Boston: Otis, Broaders and Company, 1836.

Boucher, Susan Marie, *The History of Pawtucket, 1635-1986*, The Pawtucket Public Library & The Pawtucket Centennial Committee. Printed by Arcata Graphics/Halliday Lithograph, West Hanover, MA: 1986.

Bowen, Richard LeBaron, *Early Rehoboth, Documented Historical Studies of Families and Events in This Plymouth Colony Township*, Rehoboth, MA: Privately printed 1950. Vols. II, III and IV.

Bridenbaugh, Carl, *Fat Mutton and Liberty of Conscience*, Providence, Brown University Press: 1974.

Crane, John C., *Rev. William Blackstone, The Pioneer of Boston*, Worcester, MA. Charles R. Stobbs, Printer: 1896.

Daggett, John, *A Sketch of the History of Attleborough From Its Settlement To The Division*, Edited and completed by his daughter, Amelia Daggett Sheffield, Boston: Press of Samuel Usher, 1894.

DeCosta, Rev. B. F., *William Blackstone In His Relation To Massachusetts and Rhode Island*, articles reprinted from *The Churchman* of Sept. 25 and Oct. 2, 1880.

Dow, George Francis, *Every Day Life In The Massachusetts Bay Colony*, Reprint. Originally published in Boston: 1935, Society for the Preservation of New England Antiquities. Published 1988, Dover Publications, Inc., New York.

102

Duehring, Andrew, *The Providence Journal*, Providence, June 24, 1963.

Erhardt, Dr. John G., *The History of Rehoboth, Seekonk, East Providence, Pawtucket and Barrington*, Copyright Seekonk, MA, 1982. Vols. I and II.

Evans, John Howard, *Vignettes of New England*, New York, Seabury Professional Services, a div. of The Seabury Press, 1982.

Field, Edward, *The Colonial Tavern*, Providence, 1897.

Field, Edward, editor in chief, *State of Rhode Island & Providence Plantations, A History*, The Mason Publ. & Printing Co., Boston and Syracuse, 1902. Vol. II.

Gardiner, Henry, *New England Vindication*, London, 1660, edited with notes by Charles Edward Banks, MD, printed for the Gorges Society, Portland, ME, 1884.

Gough, Robert E., *Apples From Rhode Island*, Cooperative Extension Service Bulletin 206, College of Resource Development, University of Rhode Island, 1978. 28 pages.

Green, Marcia, *The Evening Times*, Pawtucket, March 5, 1985.

Haley, John W., *The Old Stone Bank History of Rhode Island*, Vol. III, (no city, no publisher indicated) 1939.

Harris, John, *The Birth of Boston*, Boston Sunday Globe March 30, 1980, Boston.

Hopkins, Dr. Samuel, *Dictionary of National Biography*, Vol. II, Oxford, G.B.: Oxford University Press, 1917.

Howe, George, *The Tragedy Of King Philip And The Destruction of the New England Indians*, excerpt from *Mount Hope*, Viking Press, Boston.

Kraege, Elfrieda, *Life of William Blackstone*, typewritten resource document in library of Rhode Island Historical Society, Providence (undated).

Lippincott, Bertram, *Indians, Privateers and High Society*, Philadelphia and New York: J. P. Lippincott, 1961.

McGlashan, James, *History of the Blakiston Family*, Stockton, Teeside, England: John W. Baker, Printer, 1975. 36 pp.

Meharg, John H., Letter to David Balfour of Cumberland Historic District Commission dated Oct. 30, 1980.

Newman, Sylvanus Chace, *Address Delivered At The Formation Of The Blackstone Monument Association*, (Together with Preliminaries and Proceedings at Study Hill, July 4, 1855), Pawtucket: Pearce and Estey, 1855.

Newman, Sylvanus Chace, *Dexter Genealogy*, Providence: Printed by A. Crawford Greene, 1859.

Pope, Charles Henry, *The Pioneers of Maine and New Hampshire, 1623 to 1660*, Boston: Charles H. Pope, 1908.

Prince, Thomas, *A Chronological History Of New England In The Form Of Annals*, Boston: Printed by Knelland and Green for S. Gerrish, 1736, Reproduced by University Micro Film, Ann Arbor.

Ross, Marjorie Drake, *The Book of Boston*, New York: Hastings House Publishers, 1960.

Rugg, Winnifred King, *Unafraid, A Life Of Anne Hutchinson*, Boston and New York: Houghton Mifflin Co., 1930.

Russell, Howard S., *A Long, Deep Furrow, Three Centuries of Farming in New England*, Hanover, NH: University Press of New England, 1976.

Russell, Levi W., *The Native Trees of Rhode Island*, Providence: E. L. Freeman & Sons, Printers to the State, 1900. (from Annual Report 1899 of the Rhode Island State Board of Agriculture).

Sargent, L. M., orig. titled *Auld Lang Syne* and published in *The Evening Transcript*, Boston, 1849; collected and republished in booklet form titled *The Blackstone Family: Being Sketches, Biographical and Genealogical of William Blackstone and His Descendants* by Lorenzo Blackstone, Norwich, CT: *Courier office* 1857.

Shackleton, Robert, *The Book of Boston*, Philadelphia: Penn Publishing Co., 1923. p. 63

Surtees, Robert, *The History and Antiquities of the County Palatine of Durham*, London, 1823.

Tilton, Rev. George H., *A History of Rehoboth, Massachusetts, Its History for 275 Years, 1643-1918*, (Incorporates original history of the town published in 1836 by Leonard Bliss Jr.) Boston: Published by author, 1918.

Tilp, Frederick, *This Was Potomac River*, Alexandria: Published by author 1978, 1979 and 1987.

White, Elizabeth Nicholson, *Mary Barnard, Wife of Roger Williams* (no place, no date) Printer: Watchemoket Press, Inc.

White, Col. Hunter C., *Old St. Paul's In Narragansett*, Wakefield, RI: Wakefield Printing Co., 1957.

Whitehead, Russell F. and Brown, Frank Chouteau, editors; *Early Homes of Rhode Island*, (Architectual Treasures of Early America by staff of The Early American Society), Arno Press, Inc., 1977.

Woodward, Carl R., *Plantation In Yankeeland*, Wickford, RI: Publication of the Cocumscussoc Association; published by The Pequot Press, Inc., Chester, CT; Second Printing, November 1985 by Narragansett Publishing, Inc., North Kingstown, RI.

Young, Alexander, *Chronicles Of The First Planters Of The Colony Of Massachusetts Bay From 1623 to 1636*, Williamstown, MA: Corner House Publishers, 1978.

NO AUTHORS MENTIONED

.....Town Records of Attleboro, Boston, Providence and Old Colony (Plymouth).

.....*The Biographical Cyclopedia of Representative Men of Rhode Island, Providence*: National Biographical Publishing Co., 1881.

.....*Catholic Oak, Singular Ministry of the Rev. J. C. Richmond, Lonsdale,* Typewritten paper stamped "Information Desk" at Providence Public Library, 1932.

.....*Famous Men in Rhode Island.*

.....*History of the State of Rhode Island,* with illus. from original sketches, Hoag, Wade & Co., Phila.; Boston: Albert J. Wright, printer, 1878.

.....*Living Blackstones, The National Registry of, The Blackstone Family News*; Denver, 1989.

.....*Providence, Southern Gateway of New England,* Historical Publishing Co., H. A. Barker, historical director, Providence, 1926.

.....*Rhode Island and Providence Plantations, Records of the Colony Of,* State Archives, Providence.

.....*Records of Boundaries, 1737/8,* Rhode Island Archives, Providence.

.....*Massachusetts Historical Collection,* WIV, 202.

.....*Lonsdale Company, Minutes of Directors' Meetings.*

.....*Pawtucket Gazette,* May 1886, Pawtucket.

*****

ACKNOWLEDGEMENTS

A bore. That is how I looked upon the Acknowledgement page in other people's books. That was before I wrote this one. Now I know the truth. How else can I confess to the reader that I did not accomplish this work alone?

The very idea for a biography of William Blackstone came from Robert D. Billington, a member of the Blackstone River Valley National Heritage Corridor Commission and president/director of the Blackstone Valley Tourism Council. His continuing interest and that of the council's assistant to the director, Donna Houle, certainly made me realize this biography was needed and wanted.

Too, there were my computer tutors, Fire Capt. Michael Carter, Robert Carpenter and especially John E. McDevitt, Jr. It wasn't easy Boys, but you finally made it possible for me to function in the Computer Age. I am especially indebted to McDevitt's firm, JEMTECH Inc., for enabling me to present my manuscript to Heritage Books, Inc., in camera-ready form.

Then there was Phyllis Silva, retired state archivist, who gave unstintingly of her know-how, her personal interest and so much encouragement!

And there was Paul Blackstone, one of the Rev. William Blackstone's descendants now living in Branford, CT. who opened to me his treasure chest of family history. I am grateful to Frances Drouin for leading me to him.

There was Clarkson Potter who shared with me so much of his knowledge as a publisher, author, agent. I am grateful to Matt Largess for introducing us.

There was Rene Lacoste of Bowie, MD, who did much research for me in Washington, DC, area libraries. I am grateful to Marguerite Lacoste Deslauriers for putting him to work for me.

And so many more people shared facts and records and recollections with me, suggesting paths to take and giving me encouragement when I needed it most: David Balfour of the Cumberland Historic District Commission; Robert Furey and Jeanne Kennedy who worked in the Ann and Hope Mill building long, long ago; friends who loaned me old books about Rhode Island and colonial New England; and librarians whose interest and expertise gave me new respect for that profession.

To everyone who helped: Thanks.

PHOTO CREDITS

Page: Acknowledgement

6   17th century ship - AMICA Insurance greeting card

11   Rev. William Blackstone - The Pawtucket Times

13   Old English Rose - Cocumscussoc Association Pamphlet

26   Blackstone plaque - Mr. Norman Hines, Sculpter, Attleboro, MA

27   Governor Stephen Hopkins - Post card

32   Statue on Prospect terrace - RI Dept. of Economical Development

34   Richard Smith's Plantation - Cocumscussoc Association Pamphlet

37   The Catholic Oak Tree - Post card, Mr. J. Moskwa, Cumberland, RI

51   Typical kitchen fireplace - Cocumscussoc Association Pamphlet

76   John the Mariner's Grave - Louise Lind (author)

79   Ann and Hope Mill - Post card, Mr. J. Moskwa, Cumberland, RI

90   Living Blackstone relatives - Louise Lind (author)

98   Outline map of New England - Blackstone River Valley National Heritage Corridor Commission

99   Outline map of Blackstone Valley - Blackstone River Valley National Heritage Corridor Commission